I0413594

# Psychotherapy

## A Talking Cure

**Abu Sayed Zahiduzzaman**

authorHOUSE®

*AuthorHouse™*
*1663 Liberty Drive*
*Bloomington, IN 47403*
*www.authorhouse.com*
*Phone: 1 (800) 839-8640*

*© 2017 Abu Sayed Zahiduzzaman. All rights reserved.*

*No part of this book may be reproduced, stored in a retrieval system, or transmitted by any means without the written permission of the author.*

*Published by AuthorHouse 01/10/2018*

*ISBN: 978-1-5462-1579-0 (sc)*
*ISBN: 978-1-5462-1577-6 (hc)*
*ISBN: 978-1-5462-1578-3 (e)*

*Library of Congress Control Number: 2017917038*

*Print information available on the last page.*

*Any people depicted in stock imagery provided by Thinkstock are models, and such images are being used for illustrative purposes only. Certain stock imagery © Thinkstock.*

*This book is printed on acid-free paper.*

*Because of the dynamic nature of the Internet, any web addresses or links contained in this book may have changed since publication and may no longer be valid. The views expressed in this work are solely those of the author and do not necessarily reflect the views of the publisher, and the publisher hereby disclaims any responsibility for them.*

This book is dedicated to Samiya Zahiduzzaman.

# CONTENTS

# ABOUT THE AUTHOR

Abu Sayed Zahiduzzaman is 39 years old, and he likes to read and write. He has written two books: Schizophrenia: a patient's perspective and Toxic Relationship: A psychological point of view. He studied at the University of Windsor in Ontario, Canada. He majored in Psychology and graduated with a Bachelor of Arts in the year 2003. He used to play ice hockey during his Teen life, but since he got an injury at his back, he has been skating only. Since a few years, he has been passionate about photography. He enjoys taking pictures of nature and beauty. He was invited to several weddings which gave him more desire to do photography. However, he still likes to take pictures of nature and things.

# ACKNOWLEDGMENT

First of all, I send my sincere gratitude to my parents and my only one sister for reinforcing me positively to write this Book, Psychotherapy: A Talking Cure. They encouraged me continually. I want to thank my six-year old little daughter who is always happy to be with me and to spend time with me. She has been a wonderful daughter and was pleased to see me writing. I always enjoy being with her and playing games that she enjoys the most. Also, I would also like to thank my coworkers for being nice, and my boss for supporting me with kindness. Lastly, I would also like to thank Khalid Hussain (Shaheen) for designing the cover and the back pages of my book, Psychotherapy, A Talking Cure.

# ABSTRACT

This book, Psychotherapy: A Talking Cure, contains 74, 738 words and discusses Psychotherapy. It gives a briefing about the introduction to Psychotherapy. It also discusses Psychology and Harassment. Also discuss Toxic Relationship between couples, coworkers, family members, friends, and strangers. You can read about Marriage and Therapy. To those who wonder how therapists work, it will give you a snapshot of it. You can also find about the Psychology of good and evil. One may also get an idea of Counseling. By reading this book, it will help you have a better idea of various types of Attack and the Benefit of Counseling. The purpose of this writing is to inform the audiences about different types of psychotherapy, the advantage of getting counseling in time of trials or living in a difficult situation. You can investigate by reading it and discover something new. You can also use this book for your benefits and knowledge. The subject psychotherapy is so large that you have to narrow it down. However, by doing research one can tell that there are various types of therapies. You have to choose which therapy will benefit you. One can use this book as an informative way only or even used it in real life. The author of this book uses creative writing to portray his thoughts and studies.

# CHAPTER 1

# INTRODUCTION OF PSYCHOTHERAPY

It often happens in many of our day-to-day lives that we hear from friends or family that someone close to us is going to begin therapy of one sort or another. In order to understand what this implies, we must first establish a proper definition of what therapy is. For instance, one simple definition of psychotherapy is described as "the treatment of mental or emotional illness by talking about problems rather than by using medicine or drugs" (2017). On the other hand, others may define it as a treatment of mental, emotional or even physical disorders by psychological means. However, the most common medical defines it as "any alteration in an individual's interpersonal environment, relationships, or life situation brought about especially by a qualified therapist and intended to have the effect of alleviating symptoms of mental or emotional disturbance" (Merriam-Webster's Learner's Dictionary, 2016). It is also commonly known as therapy through conversation.

Different people have different opinions of psychotherapy, and many of us may wonder whether it is really efficient, or if it even works at all. Most experts in health-related fields will agree that it helps to a certain extent. There are enough resources out there to help individuals feel better and improve their overall health.

However, bettering oneself cannot solely come from external sources; it must come from within. One needs to accept that there will always be some days that are better than others. No one is ever one hundred percent healthy, and here are many factors that can affect health. Drops in overall health are normal and happen to everyone. Flus, fevers, colds, coughs, or other small illnesses are events in life that are to be taken in stride.

However, some people may develop concern by some of these symptoms and may choose to undergo psychotherapy as a result.

In the following paragraphs and pages, I will describe and talk about psychotherapy in more depth. My hope in writing this book is that you, as the reader, will develop a better sense of understanding of what psychotherapy is, and consequently use this book as a source of knowledge in your life and in the life of those around you.

## What is psychology?

Psychology – from the Greek word meaning "breath, spirit, and soul" - is the scientific study of human and animal mind and behavior. In psychology, we study the thought process, mental process, the brain, emotions, feelings, memories, reasoning, language, dreams, evolution of species, life development, biology, criminal investigation, and the way we think through different methods of research. Humans study such areas as human development, sports, health, clinical, social behavior and cognitive processes.

## What is psychiatry?

A psychiatrist is a medical doctor who has specialized in mental health and mental disorders. Oftentimes a psychiatrist is an expert in addiction, anxiety, behaviour, cognition, depression, emotion, mania, mood, psychosis, perceptions, and various other fields. Their practice often focuses on the diagnoses and treatment of mental illnesses.

## What is Psychotherapy?

Psychotherapy is a practice performed by psychologists that is used to assist patients with mental issues. Both psychologists and registered, qualified counselors, practice psychotherapy, which uses various approaches in healing including: cognitive-behavioral therapy and interpersonal therapy, among others, to treat individual patients based on their unique backgrounds and concerns. The treatment is based on the ground relationship between clients or patients with psychologists or counselors, and helps one to be free of discussion in an open dialogue with someone that can provide an environment that helps you to communicate openly with one who is objective, nonjudgmental, and neutral. By analyzing your mental states, thoughts, and behavior, one can help you solve the very issues that prompted you to begin a session in the first place. One will help you develop with skills and challenges that were in the past, from present to future.

"Psychotherapy is a professional practice regulated by laws in Quebec. The Bill 21 gives an accurate definition of psychotherapy. It is a "psychological treatment for a mental disorder, behavioral disturbance or other problem resulting in psychological suffering or distress, and has as its purpose to foster significant changes in the client's cognitive, emotional or behavioral functioning, interpersonal relations, personality or health. Such treatment goes beyond help aimed at dealing with everyday difficulties and beyond a support or counselling role." (2017)." There are many types of psychotherapy: for individuals, couples, and families. Anyone can benefit from ps psy·cho·ther·a·py and it pronounce as *n. pl.* psy·cho·ther·a·pies.

## Where does psychotherapy come from?

According to Tyrrell., M. (2003)., the origins of psychotherapy date from 3,500 years ago in ancient Egyptian and Greek writing. The terminology "Counselling" or "Psychotherapy" simply mean "helping someone using psychological means". The word counselling was used as early as 1386 in Chaucer's Wife of Bath's Tale (Tyrrell, 2003). In the Western domains, Orientalists have noted that "Sufi literature is full of evidence of profound psychological insight and sophisticated psychotherapeutic procedures. Historical Sufis such as Jalaludin Rumi of Afghanistan and El Ghazali of Persia display psychological understandings which have only recently been paralleled in the West". This practice has existed has since for many years through verbal communication, in one form or another.

## Branches of psychotherapy

There are many distinctions between branches of psychotherapy, but these may not be so blatant to people unfamiliar with the topic as it is for health professionals. There are many different branches of psychotherapy in the world. This is why I will only discuss a select few in this book.

For example, the following is an alphabetically ordered list of a variety of types of therapy practiced today: art therapy, attack therapy, behavior therapy, chess therapy, child therapy, dance therapy, drama therapy, emotional focus therapy, expressive therapy, family therapy, feminist therapy, Freudian psychotherapy, Gestalt therapy, group therapy, hypnotherapy, interpersonal therapy, Jungian psychotherapy, logo therapy, marriage therapy, music therapy, narrative therapy, nude psychotherapy, parent-child therapy, psychodynamic psychotherapy, reality therapy, relationship counselling, sex therapy, social therapy, and many more. Surprisingly enough, each country has their own types of therapy, but some popular ones are recurring in many countries. The following paragraphs will go into more detail about the different types of therapy.

## Art therapy

Art therapy can be understood as a way of expressing oneself mentally, emotionally, and physically when going through a difficult time. It is a type of therapy that is used to explore oneself creatively. Doing something artistic can be beneficial to developing one's skills and thus helping one achieve their goals by reducing stress, overcoming self-esteem issues, and controlling their own behavior and feelings.

Some people enjoy drawing or panting while others enjoy activities such as sculpting, all depending on their own qualities and talents. For some, coloring books are great stress reducers. Being a professional artist is definitely not a requirement for undergoing art therapy.

Of course, different people will have different talents, and these are explored in this type of therapy. That said, everyone can benefit in some way or other from this type of therapy. It has different outcomes depending on the person in question. However, most people will find that it helps them heal, treat, and rehabilitate themselves.

Usually, art therapists have knowledge in a wide array of psychological theories; some may have clinical practice, while others may take a more spiritual approach to therapy. There are therapists who focus on certain age groups, while others cater to all ages, and with entirely different circumstances. Art therapists usually work in wellness centers, schools, hospitals, rehabilitation centers, medical institutions, nursing homes, or in private practices. One of the main advantages of art therapy is that anyone can express themselves in various ways.

## Behavior therapy

According to Kristeen Cherney (2013), behavior therapy is defined as "a treatment that helps change potentially self-destructing behaviors. It is also called behavioral modification or cognitive behavioral therapy (CBT). Medical professionals use this type of therapy to replace bad habits with good ones. The therapy also helps people cope with difficult situations. It is most often used to treat anxiety disorders. However, one does not need to be diagnosed with a mental health disorder to benefit from this kind of therapy". Behavior therapy can be used to treat illnesses such as schizophrenia, bipolar disorder, depression, social phobia, and to help those who have to live alongside people with these disorders. This therapy can be also very useful for someone who has autism, substance abuse, a personality disorder or an eating disorder. Behavior therapy is a really important type of therapy in our society. Many different techniques can be recommended to patients to help them cope with a variety of situations. For example, some such techniques include breathing exercises, journal writing, or meditation. Some medical professionals also suggest positive thinking and positive reinforcement, as well as daily exercise. Feelings of pain, fear, and anger are often targeted by these recommendations. One of the great benefits of this kind of therapy is developing an increased ability to cope with the stresses of life. The main goal of behavior therapy is to acquire a better understanding of oneself and the available treatments. Behavior therapy is a learning process that helps patients deal more effectively with their moods and their emotions. The greater investment one puts into therapy, the greater reward they receive. There is nothing to lose when undergoing behavior therapy, there is only knowledge to be gained. The most important is that the patient finds ways of healing themselves and feeling better overall.

My advice to you is to boost your motivation. Attend all the sessions that the medical expert schedules. Greater involvement leads to greater recovery. After all, everything will depend on you. The healing system is there for you, and you need to use it. How fast you heal will depend on if you really want to feel better and continue your journey all the way through. Using this therapy will help you in your daily life. It is not a cure but a way for each individual to get better gradually.

## Chess therapy

What can be said about chess therapy? It is quite common to see people playing chess, but chess therapy is less well-known. Chess is a fun game that was created in Asia. According to Wikipedia, Chess History "the most commonly held belief is that chess originated in India, where it was called Chaturanga, which appears to have been invented in the 6th century AD. Although this is commonly believed, it is thought that Persians created a more modern version of the game after the Indians" (2016).

It is one of the most famous games around the world that people play. It is a game that requires two players. The game can last anywhere from a few minutes to many hours. Some players even choose to play each move once a day, others once a week, and some even once a month. Some chess games can go on for years. Depending on your opponent, chess can be fun and entertaining or long and tiring. It is a game that requires deep thinking, calm emotions, patience, and acceptance. The game requires thinking out each move to achieve the ultimate goal of putting your opponent in a "check mate", where he or she can no longer play.

In order to think clearly, emotions need to be controlled and balanced, otherwise performance can be easily affected. Therefore, this game could take many hours to play, depending on the players. Nowadays, there are chess clocks that time each player's turn to ensure that moves are played in a timely manner. If one player exceeds the time, then the other player wins automatically. This game is very strategic and helps develop your mind.

Today in Quebec, Canada, chess is introduced to elementary and high school. The main goal of this introduction is to get students to think differently and interact with others from different cultural backgrounds.

The game of chess is simple in theory. It is played between two opponents on opposite sides of a board containing 64 squares of alternating colors. Each player has 16 pieces: 1 king, 1 queen, 2 rooks, 2 bishops, 2 knights, and 8 pawns. The goal of the game is to checkmate the other king.

According to Dr. Angelo Subida (2014), a psychotherapist who has a private clinic in the Philippines, chess therapy can help people overcome certain mental health issues. According to him "chess therapy is now used by numerous psychotherapists and doctors. It has become a popular creative psychotherapy technique in the past 20 years. This therapy has been known to produce positive results with children who have bipolar disorders, depression, ADHD, and neuro-behavioral disorders." This type of therapy is great for people with certain kinds of mental illness. Chess therapy is a creative form of therapy used to develop bonds between the psychotherapist and his/her clients. According to Dr. Angelo Subida, (2014), "chess therapy was founded as early as AD 852-932 by a certain Dr. Rhazes who was chief physician at Baghdad Hospital. Dr. Rhazes uses chess strategies and tactics as metaphors in real life to help patients think clearer".

## Child therapy

Being a child can be very difficult. Some children have a hard time just being a child, whereas, it is also difficult to be a good parent. What happens when some children need more attention than others, or what happens when parents need more attention than others? Parenting is important and most of all, parents want the best for their children. One way to know if children need more attention is to observe their behaviour when they start to go to school. Parents usually want their children to have the best education. Teachers can usually help detect a child who has a disability.

A child may show signs of learning difficulties early on while others may develop problems over time. Early detection is best. Your child might have dyslexia, learning disability or ADHD or others types of illness. A child may be seen as intelligent to some, but not to others.

Does your child need to work very hard to get better grades in school? Is he or she struggling a lot to get the passing grade or is the child taking a lot of your time to do their homework? Do you help them daily with their extra work at home? Do teachers call often or complain about having a hard time completing their tasks at school? Can you see that your child does not put enough effort at school or spend more time playing rather than doing homework? There are many questions that can be asked but you need to find the time to figure out the answers. Child therapy is one way of getting answers. Teachers can evaluate each child with various types of tests. Your child's academic level and cognitive development can be examined in order for your child to be helped during his years at school. Strengths and weaknesses can be revealed through these tests and recommendations can be made to improve the situation as well as the grades of the child. Some children may show signs of struggles while developing their language skills. Regular assessments help psychotherapists monitor educational progress. It is wise to see a psychologist or a therapist when your child is not listening to you, or when your child seeks negative attention. Sometimes, your child may even disrupt other children by using force or screaming, developing negative bonds with other children around. You do not know what to do or how to behave with your child? You need to find a solution and maybe contact a therapist. Having problems with your child can also damage your relationship with your spouse and sometimes your surroundings. It is possible to change your child's behavior without punishing him or her. Therapists can guide you to better manage your stress and find solutions to cope with your suffering child. What happens when your child has anxiety? Your child may cry often or scream, feel sad, be angry, be afraid or may even be unable to sleep at night. In order to help your child overcome his or her problems, you will need to better manage your own behavior. Having problems with low self-esteem can cause brain damage in children. They may give up very quickly and have trouble understanding daily routine or tasks. He or she may feel shy and need to be pushed to do any activities. Children need to believe in themselves and a parent needs to help them thrive in that area. You can do this by reminding them of things they have already accomplished and succeeded at before. Do this often and gradually they will become more and more confident to undertake projects and set goals on their own. When children feel pride in what they do, their sense of self-worth is strengthened. Eventually, this habit helps children lead productive lives.

What happens when your child reaches adolescence? At this stage of development, teenagers like to explore various things and experiment with others in order to build their identity. Self-esteem is at stake for adolescents. Some of the basic things most adolescents go through are complaints about not being attractive, feeling left-out or lonely, rejected from a group, not understanding romance and therefore confusing attraction and lust with real love. They also do not know and have not yet learned how to deal with new emotions, sensations or feelings they have never experienced before. Their minds, bodies and souls being overwhelmed by rapid transformation, it is no surprise if confused teenagers often do not make sound decisions. They may feel anxious and some have suicidal thoughts. Parents need to help and be there for their adolescents in crisis. Parents play an important role in their adolescents' lives. Children may need more therapy if their parents separate. It is a very rough time for both parents and even harder for their children.

Children may go through various stages of feelings in these situations. Coping with children is also very difficult during times of divorce. Children have two different homes and perhaps new step-parents if their mother or father marries someone else. When parents divorce, teenagers go through various situations that require parental attention. They may have problems at school or may not sleep or eat well. From one moment to the next, they may become sad or very moody. As a parent, if you have a new partner, it may cause more problems with your child. Some step-parents do not get along well with their new step-children. It might be difficult to adjust to the surroundings and some even feel ashamed that their parents are divorced.

## Dance movement therapy

Wikipedia (2016) cites Dance movement therapy as "Dance/movement therapy (DMT) in USA/ Australia or dance movement psychotherapy (DMP) in the UK is the psychotherapeutic use of movement and dance to support intellectual, emotional, and motor functions of the body. As a form of expressive therapy, DMT looks at the correlation between movement and emotion".

In the "Les Grands Ballets Canadiens de Montreal (2016)" section, we read how DMT came to be.

"Dance/movement therapy (DMT) first emerged in the United States in the 1940s, when various pioneers developed methods based on diverse approaches to bodily movement. It is used either as a complement to various medical or psychotherapeutic treatments".

The main purpose of DMT is to promote the health and well-being of individuals. One may ask how to become a dance movement therapist. According to the international standards set in place by associations delivering dance/movement therapy accreditations, it is necessary to have completed a graduate university training including clinical psychology and dance/movement therapy (DMT) courses in order to access a dance/movement therapist accreditation. It is necessary for the body and mind to move. In order to be healthy we should practice dance movement therapy. Most of us love to dance, so why not dance for fun or just for therapy purpose?

When in movement, our body is constantly moving and the mind is adjusting to the movement as well. It is a form of exercise. The more we exercise the better is for our health. Obviously, we should not overdo it but just so we are fit and comfortable with DMT. Doing exercise like dancing is always good for the body and mind. It is also a stress releaser. You will realize that after dancing you may be out of breath that you need to rest. This is why DMT can promote a state of relaxation. It helps people achieving emotional, cognitive, physical, and social integration.

Beneficial for both physical and mental health, dance therapy can be used for stress reduction, disease prevention, and mood management. Dancing is a unique way of maximizing your health. When you are healthy you have more control of yourself and you are in better shape to do various activities; you acquire strength to achieve what you want in life. Doing Dance movement therapy will give you more hope and better mastery of your body. It might boost your self-esteem. Some people may like to listen to music, others sing while listening to music, other dance when they want and are enjoying every moment of their life by listening to music and doing Dance movement therapy.

What is the main function of a Dance movement therapist one might ask? Well, Dance Movement therapists work with all types of people (groups, families, communities and all age group). Their role is to improve people's self-esteem and body image and also to help them better communicate by improving their relational skills. Therapists expand people's movement vocabulary and show them how to cope with various social interactions. Therapists are in demands for research, assessment, observation, therapeutic interaction and intervention. Dance Movement therapists work with various groups such as health care centers, crises centers, medical institutes, counseling centers, drug treatment centers, nursing home, schools, rehabilitation centers, and also psychiatric wards. A dance movement therapist must obtain a Master's Degree in order to practice professionally. The therapist and clients can create a unique way to explore dance and movement beneficial to both of them.

**Drama therapy**

The main function of Drama therapy is to achieve goals through the art of storytelling, facilitating the uncovering and ultimately the expression of feelings and thoughts in order to resolve issues and achieve catharsis. This therapy is dynamic. It uses drama and theater to promote personal transformation. It can be practiced by all segments of population. This therapy helps people grow emotionally and achieve some personal goals. One's ego can be developed by this approach, which also promotes psychological integration, social skills and behavior transformation. It has the potential to improve the quality of life as it develops the ability to resolve problems and overcome challenges in life. The intention of a

Drama therapist is to help people with a range of mental issues, cognitive and development disorders. They learn to express themselves through the creative use of their body and voice, discovering along the way their strengths and weaknesses. Drama therapy favors the learning and exploration of the deepest feelings in the body and mind by role playing such as a lover, a son, daughter, parents, wife, husband, boss, friends, and strangers. The different characters will help better understand various relationships in daily life. Each session explores various theatre techniques such as enactment, theatrical games, storytelling and improvisation.

Furthermore, Jacob L. Moreno's therapeutic approach called psychodrama, also known as srama therapy, "uses guided dramatic action to address issues and concerns" (2017). Early drama therapy contributors include Nikolai Evreinov, Vladimir Iljne, Bertholt Brecht, Sandor Ferenczi, Neva Boyd, and Constantin Stanislavski. Other contributors, sharing influences from role theory, analytical psychology, and creative arts therapies, propelled the field from "theater as therapy" to what we now call drama therapy. They include theorists and professionals like Peter Slade, Carl Jung, T. D. Noble, Winifred Ward, Maxwell Jones, Gertrud Schattner, and Sue Jennings".

The main goals of therapists are to ensure that people realize that they need support and some sort of help. "Drama therapy continues to gain ground as a treatment modality. It can be used in a variety of settings, including schools, mental health clinics, prisons, hospitals, and community centers. Drama therapy may be used as a treatment for the following: posttraumatic stress, anxiety, depression, interpersonal relationship issues, substance abuse, behavioral issues related to autism, rehabilitation, schizophrenia, dementia, eating disorders, learning difficulties, grief and loss" (Good therapy org. 2017). If you go experience some of the above illnesses, you should seek help.

## Emotionally- focused therapy

The purpose of Emotional focus therapy (EFT) is to help people better identify their emotions. Trusting is a key word for the EFT therapists as they will guide and give hope to couples to better adapt and channel their emotions from painful memories that have become maladaptive to them and wish to change their belief system. Therapy helps patient develop their empathy.

In the Good Therapy Organization (2017), website, Gerald Corey lists the following steps in emotionally-focused therapy:

"Stage One: Cycle De-escalation

Step 1:   Identify key issues of concern.

Step 2:   Identify ways negative patterns of interaction increase conflict when key issues arise.

Step 3:   The therapist assists in the identification of unacknowledged fears and negative emotions related to attachment underlying negative interaction patterns.

Step 4:   The therapist reframes key issues for the couple in terms of negative patterns of interaction, underlying emotions and fears, and each individual's attachment needs.

Stage Two: Changing Interaction Patterns

Step 5:   Individuals are assisted in voicing both their attachment needs and deep emotions.

Step 6:    Partners are coached in ways to express acceptance and compassion for a Partner's attachment needs and deep emotions.

Step 7:   Partners are coached in the expression of attachment needs and emotions while also learning ways to discuss those issues likely to cause conflict.

Stage Three: Consolidation and Integration

Step 8:   The therapist coaches the couple in the use of new communication styles to talk about old problems and develop new solutions.

Step 9:   The couple learns ways to use skills practiced in therapy outside of session and develops a plan to make new interaction patterns a consistent part of life after therapy" (06-30- 2016).

The Emotional focused therapy is a kind of family therapy. The therapy is an essential therapy that help people with various attachments, steps and stages. The clients develop with their family members how to approach and trust each other for better emotional bond. Researchers have proven that

Emotional focused therapy work and help one each other based on how the relationship have distress and success. The therapy decreases distress within relationships and partners interact in more successful ways. It is shown that the outcome of the therapy is more positive and encouraging.

**Expressive therapy**

Expressive therapy, also known as expressive arts therapy or creative arts therapy, is the use of the creative arts as a form of therapy. Some would say that the expressive therapy is related to drama therapy or music therapy. There are various ways of seeing expressive therapy: some would say that it incorporates music, painting, drawing, movement, dance, drama or even writing.

Therapies may help people understand their responses, internal or external reactions through sounds, pictures, exploration in an art process. To benefit from art expressive therapy, you do not need to have artistic qualification or talents or ability. It is simple and easy to do. You just need to participate and be willing to explore yourself. The process of the therapy is mainly to seek meaning, clarity and healing. As each person is unique, this therapy will help everyone in a different way. People may use various types of therapy such as movement, journaling or a combination of the two. Usually, patients have low skill and are very sensitive. With time, therapists help individuals determine their strengths and rhythms. People who go through depression, anxiety, eating disorders, or who have social challenges are recommended to go through the therapy.

Nowadays, people use finger painting, mask making or other types of craft as therapeutic means of healing. Depending on each person, the technique used is different. The therapist may suggest something but you have to listen to yourself during therapy. For example, the therapist may tell you to paint what is meaningful to you. The therapist will not say which colors to use or which painting style to use, it has to come from yourself and you have to use your own judgment. The expressive art therapy focuses basically on a few major guidelines, such as connecting with yourself, using your imagination, following your heart and observing yourself. You may wonder what takes to become an expressive arts therapist; well, in order to train, one has to have at least master's degree in counseling with a focus in expressive arts therapy. Others go on to have a PhD. However, there is no evidence to show where healing comes from with this type of therapy; the therapist or the patient.

## Family therapy

All families face challenges at some point in their lives. These challenges can be a source of growth of learning if well managed. Not everyone may know how to handle difficult situations, such as managing a child with a disability, or being a parent in general. Sometimes, parents may not know how to handle their teenagers or may have a hard time communicating with them. This can therefore make life difficult for couples and may create conflict. Parenting is difficult, and it is even more difficult to build a strong relationship between husbands, wives, and their children.

Relationships can be hard to build and easy to break. Broken relationships and divorce can take a large toll on families. There are resources out there that can be of help, such as therapists, who are there to enhance communication between couples, or between parents and their children. They help find strategies to reduce conflict at home and in society at large. Therapists help family members understand each other better. They can also help manage the transition between divorce and remarriage. Therapy can be done solo or as a group, in cases of family therapy.

Being in a relationship is not the same for everyone. Some people feel secure in their relationships, whereas others may feel more insecure in a couple than they might on their own. Trust and admiration are key for successful relationships. Most humans seek someone who will be understanding of them and who will comfort them in their relationship. Love, intimacy, and passion are also top priorities when seeking a suitor. However, even in relationships that have all these qualities, tensions develop, or it becomes clear that something is lacking. When this happens, both individuals should seek help from a therapist if they want their relationship to work. Despite some preconceived ideas, there is nothing wrong in getting support from a professional.

Romantic relationships differ from parent-child relationships. There is also a lot of variety among child-raising habits. Some parents are more punitive then others, depending on what they best for them and their children. However, there is a point at which being hard on one's children is doing more harm than good. Being firm yet gentle is arguable the best approach to child-raising. Disobedience is common among young children as they grow. Every child or teenager experiences something different as they grow up and go through school. Children react differently to their environment. This is why conversing with children is important; that is how parents can truly understand their personalities. Most parents wish their children would be more disciplined, but this is not the reality. Children need freedom and space to move and to grow.

Some parents use divinity as a source of therapy. They train their children to become very religious, some are successful, others are not.

Although not all children need all the same things, most children need a sense of stability and bonding with their parents. What can cause a family to break up? There are many reasons, of course, but firstly, bad stress management can be a cause of divorce. Secondly, bad communication can easily exacerbate problems. Thirdly, poor division of labor can lead to a sense of injustice between individuals, which then causes conflict. Differing money management habits or respect for money can also create tensions between partners.

Fourthly, and obviously, cheating can create severe stress in a relationship. Honesty is key to a successful relationship. Purity and holiness is associated to families that consist two married parents with children.

A less obvious trigger for divorce can be, indirectly, children. If children have problems in school, social issues, anxiety, or behavioral problems, parents may feel added stress and it may affect their relationship as a consequence. It is important as parents to give each other a chance to breathe.

Sometimes, a second marriage can cause problems. However, it is important to remember that there is an answer to everything. Worrying is toxic to any relationship; rather, partners should seek to take action as soon as possible.

Finances can be an additional source of stress, and can ruin a relationship. Any source of stress, be it of financial nature or other, can lead to lack of sleep. Although this might not be common knowledge, recurring lack of sleep can lead to relationship stress, and eventually, break up.

Hopefully the above paragraphs have served to enlighten you, the reader, as to why families may have problems, and thus help you guide your own energies. Of course, all crises are difficult to live through, and that is why many types of therapy are there to help. Believe in yourself, and believe in your partner, and if you have children, just remember that you are both parents. Give yourselves a break. If you are a step-parent, give a chance to your new partner's and his or her children. After all, building a family is the most valuable thing on Earth and it is something to be treasured.

## Feminist therapy

Since 1960 in many countries, feminist therapy exploded and women sought more than ever to educate and develop themselves through it. By the late 1960's it evolved into feminist psychology and the beginning of the widespread feminist movement. Women were encouraged to be strengthened in many areas such as assertiveness, communication, relationship, self-esteem and most importantly, education. Women and men alike acquired knowledge in feminist therapy.

The main goal was to develop an equal and mutual relationship of caring and support. This therapy is not exclusive to women because men can also benefit from it. It helps individuals sort out personal experiences embedded in political situations, contexts, and social realities. Feminist therapy also focuses on empowering women by helping them see the impact of gender issues such as sex roles in society, minority status and socialization as possible sources or causes of psychological difficulties. The core concept is equality; therefore, the therapist is seen as equal in the relationship among men and women. Men also deal with social and gender role constraints such as the demands of strength, autonomy, and competition. Men can benefit from therapy by working on these issues and by learning new skills to help them understand and explore issues involved with emotions, intimacy, and self-disclosure.

There are four major approaches that are unique to feminist therapy which include consciousness-raising, social and gender role analysis, socialization, and social activism. The definition of consciousness-raising is when there is activism of any kind by a group of people who attempt to attract the attention of a larger segment of society to a specific cause or condition. Social and gender role analysis involves the evaluation of a person's psychological distress and methods of coping. Moreover, socialization refer to the lifelong process of inheriting and disseminating norms, customs, values and ideologies, providing an individual with the skills and habits necessary to function in his society. Fourthly, social activism is an intentional action with the goal of bringing about social change. Many people run in politics in order to change social issues into positive transformations.

There are four main philosophies of feminism with differing goals in therapy including socialist, radical, cultural, and liberal. First of all, the socialist feminism focus on the need for change in social relationship and functional. Second, radical feminism is based on the need of changing the gender relationship and common tradition. Thirdly, cultural feminism points out to the importance of recognition for women who are devalued in our modern society and how there are disadvantaged. Lastly, liberal feminism focuses on the biases of people in order to promote self-awareness, self-respect, self-esteem and equal rights between men and women. Mostly, the main idea behind feminism is that women and men should be considered as equal.

According to Gerald Corey (2007), feminist therapy is based on five interrelated principles:

1. The personal is political which implements social change.
2. The counseling relationship is egalitarian which encourages equality between the therapist and the client. The client should be aware that she has the power to change and define herself and the therapist is only a tool with new insight and information.
3. Women's experiences are honored and they should get in touch with their personal experiences and intuition.
4. Definitions of distress and mental illness are reformulated involving the internal as well as external factors of distress. Pain and resistance are viewed as a positive confirmation of the desire to live and overcome distress rather than being viewed as weak.
5. Feminist therapists use an integrated analysis of oppression which means that they understand that both men and women are subjected to oppression and stereotypes and that these oppressive experiences have a profound effect on beliefs and perceptions." On a particular website (Good Therapy Org. 2017), various people express comments on feminism and feminist therapy. The following comments are from people who have expressed their opinion on the subject:

Elsa from Ontario, believes it means that "men and women should be treated the same way, and boys should help women accomplish that".

Lana from Ontario states that "it means finding the courage to never stop building a more inclusive world".

Khursheed from Ontario, believes that "it means not being afraid to stand up for the rights and freedoms of half of humanity".

Rocio from Mexico says to "fight for what is fair, make choices in freedom and not conform".

Celia from Ontario, states that feminism "means recognizing the equality of the sexes, of fighting to keep society fair and equal to all, regardless of what sex an individual was born as or identifies as".

Denise from Ontario believes we need to "acknowledge the world systemic oppression of women and girls, and fight for their empowerment".

Susan from Ontario, states, "it means valuing all human being in the same way regardless of their physical appearance".

Romik from Manitoba, states, "as a male feminist, it means to learn, listen, and try and do my part (as small as it may be) to help the movement".

Elsii from Canada, believes you need to have "the ability to be your authentic self".

Emily from Ontario, encourages the "empowerment of women to create inclusive and supportive space for all genders.

Ale from Ontario, believes "in equal rights for everyone".

The main concept here is to focus on establishing equal rights between men and women. For many centuries, men overruled women. In majority of the countries, men are in charge of governing the country. In many sectors, men run and rule departments. Men in many areas are the main ideologists. To this day in some countries, men dominate women. However, this concept has radically changed over time. Women became enlightened with high ambition, their own beliefs, self-awareness, and self-centeredness. Women wished to have power, they show hunger for power and many are on the same level as many men. Now, in most continents, they are seen as equal to men. Women have always been powerful beings, however, it has never been acknowledged adequately in many cultures. Obviously, some women ruled in the past but we see women taking the lead more and more. For a man, it can be nice to see their wives taking care of them. Women play an important role in our modern society and in the future they will still play an important role. Will we see more women taking care of our countries? There is always room to reach the top. When you love someone, such as a woman, you do not need to worry because your love is true and you will feel that your woman is true to you. Both genders need the other in order to live together harmoniously.

## Freudian psychotherapy

Sigmund Freud was born in Austria on May 6, 1856 and died on September 23, 1939. He was a physician specialized in neurology. The founder of psychoanalysis, Sigmund Freud is known worldwide as the father of psychology. His name appears in most books on the subject of psychology and students of that discipline, as well as the general population, are familiar with his work and research on the subconscious mind. One of the main ideas that he brought forth was that

"…unconscious motives control much behavior that particular kinds of unconscious thoughts and memories, especially sexual and aggressive ones, are the source of neurosis, and that neurosis could be treated through bringing these unconscious thoughts and memories to consciousness in psychoanalytic treatment (Freud, Sigmund | Internet Encyclopedia of Philosophy, 2015).

Sigmund was very interested in hypnotism and came to believe that it was useful to treat mental illness. Hypnosis is at the core of psychoanalysis. Initially interested in what was then called conversion syndrome, he eventually expanded his work to other forms of neurosis, especially obsessive-compulsive disorders. His theory is based on human behavior and human mind, with a clinical approach. As a neurologist, Freud published many medical papers on the subject of cerebral paralysis. Based on his research, he provided strong scientific techniques for therapy which were later used to bring to the conscious mind repressed thoughts and feeling.

According to the Theory of Personality website (2015). "Sigmund Freud's psychoanalytic theory of personality argues that human behavior is the result of the interactions among three component parts of the mind: the id, ego, and superego.

This "structural theory" of personality places great importance on how conflicts among the parts of the mind shape behavior and personality. These conflicts are mostly unconscious.

According to Freud, personality develops during childhood and is critically shaped through a series of five psychosexual stages, which he called his psychosexual theory of development.

During each stage, a child is presented with a conflict between biological drives and social expectations; successful navigation of these internal conflicts will lead to mastery of each developmental stage, and ultimately to a fully mature personality.

Freud's ideas have since been met with criticism, in part because of his singular focus on sexuality as the main driver of human personality development"

The main focus of psychoanalysis is to identify and interpret dreams, as well as detect free associations between words as well as images. Freud would encourage his clients to develop insight about their own behavior and find the meaning behind personal symbols. Basically, he studied the phenomenon of repressed emotions and forgotten experiences and sought ways to explain and link the unconscious causes of impulses, anxieties and internal conflicts. The Freudian approach to human understanding probes into early childhood all the way to adulthood. This therapy is known to be a very long process, from a few weeks to a few years, depending on the subject's response and particular circumstances. The main goal is to promote personal and emotional growth through insight from one's own personal past in a judgment-free environment provided by the therapist.

## Gestalt therapy

In 1940s, Fritz Perls, Laura Perls and Paul Goodman developed a new therapy called Gestalt therapy. *Gestalt* is a German word meaning shape or form. It is based on experiential and humanistic therapy. Gestalt therapy aims at enriching one's creativity in order to enhance awareness, self-direction and freedom.

The main purpose of Gestalt therapy is to help people develop understanding, empathy and unconditional acceptance. In order to do so, it is essential to understand self and map one's own personal history. With this outlook, one can go through psychotherapy and achieve this objective by letting the therapists know what they have on their mind. Being truthful towards the therapist or even to self is really important during the therapeutic process. Equally important in Gestalt therapy is to recognize that forcing a person to change against his or her own conviction usually results in a negative outcome. With this in mind, both client and therapist can progress together as they meet regularly and develop an approach conducive to trust and understanding so that the client is able to open up and share his or her true feelings and thoughts.

This therapy focuses mainly on the present time and particular context the client is experiencing. Learning to control suppressed feelings and impulsions while accepting and trusting emotions is the goal of Gestalt therapy. More precisely, it aims at increasing awareness of self in the here and now, without neglecting the impact of past experiences as well as one's outlook on the future. The main goal of the therapist is to make an individual understand what factors shaped a particular memory by bringing up the present moment or how the present moment is influenced by experiences of the past.

Developing new creative approaches during the therapy are very much recommended. Therapists are not given any specific guidelines to follow; they can make a session very organized and structured or casual and even entertaining. The goal is to make the individual feel comfortable according to his personality. Always focusing on the here and now, questions are asked and directed at the client to help him or her to realize where he or she stands. This is how the individual is trained to increase his awareness of self and leads to a better understanding of how he personally experiences the present moment.

The sessions are simple, based on experimentations and exercises which can be done one on one or within a group. The therapists usually designed their session mainly to make the person in therapy arouse emotions and actions.

The sessions are also based on understanding different aspects of a conflict, experience, or mental health issue. The therapist may also ask the person in therapy to do various types of exercises, such as a repeated and exaggerate movements like bouncing a leg when feeling a particular emotion in order to bring awareness of one's behavior during the session. Such exercises lead an individual to reconnect with parts of themselves they may minimize, ignore, or deny. Depending on each individual, a session with a gestalt therapist yields unique results. Until you try something new you will never know if it can help you.

## Group therapy

Group therapy consists of attending a therapy session managed either by a psychologist, psychiatrist, social worker or qualified therapist, in a group of three to twenty people at the same time. Group therapy is a form of psychotherapy. Sometimes, when the group is too large there can be sub-groups to better assist each person who needs social support. This type of therapy is widely available at a variety of locations including private therapeutic practices, hospitals, mental health clinics, and community centers, or even in the workplace.

Attending group therapy gives hope and boosts self-esteem. Being surrounded by other people helps one realize that they are not alone in a difficult situation. Obviously, everybody has unique issues but it can help to be with someone rather than being alone. Often, when one feels lonely in a particularly difficult situation, it is easy to become isolated; however, when in group therapy, people often feel hope and companionship. Sometimes, it feels good to hold someone else's hand. In group therapy, participants share personal information. As you share your sorrow and worry, another person may have insight or advice that has the potential to make you feel better and boost your confidence. For some, their group acts as a family. Friendships are developed and similar beliefs are shared, helping those involved. Each participant can explore their beliefs or childhood experiences while being supported by the group and in turn support the others. Based on behavior during the therapy, the participants can point out destructive patterns seen in each other in order to improve situations and provide guidance. This type of socialization can be a solution for some. It can be a new beginning as it opens doors to trustworthy relationships. Typical group therapy lasts 15 to 20 weeks and sometimes longer; in some cases, up to ten years.

Group therapy calls for a willingness to let others know about oneself in spite of one's reluctance, in order to trade past failure for a more successful outlook and way of thinking and being. A sense of belonging and acceptance grows as the participants get to know each other. Therapists are there to support the efforts of the group both collectively and individually. They lead each session by acknowledging progress as well as pitfalls in the behaviors of the participants and offer their insight in order to promote personal growth. They facilitate the exchange between participants. The group also provides valuable feedback to each individual. Sharing feelings and experiences with a group of people can help relieve pain, guilt, or stress. Group therapy helps the participants realize that they are responsible for their own lives, actions, and choices.

There are many special group therapies tailored for the individual in need of support. Here is a list of types of therapy that can be offered within a group: Conflict between couple and families, separation and divorce issues, relational difficulties, self-esteem issues, relationship issues, depression, parenting skills training, social phobias, anger management, stress management, behavior management, panic attacks, insomnia, empowerment, eating disorders, grief and loss, trauma, OCD (Obsessive-compulsive disorder), post-traumatic disorder (PTSD), and general anxiety. The sessions can be offered once or twice a week for usually an hour each session, sometimes less, depending on the participants and the therapist. Each individual shares information with the therapist, who in turn will provide help, guidance and advice on a daily basic. There will always be ups and downs but with time it is possible to see improvement. Patience and full participation in the task asked by the therapist eventually pays off.

There are usually two different types of sessions, either open or closed. Open sessions allow new participants to join the group spontaneously and are welcomed by the therapist. On the other hand, closed sessions have a fixed number of participants for the duration of the therapy. The meeting room is arranged in a way that everybody can face each other, and the chairs are put in a circle to promote equality between the participants. The sessions start with greetings followed by a time when each participant shares his or her daily routine.

How effective is group therapy? Studies have shown that group therapy can be an effective treatment for depression and traumatic stress disorders. It also helps with other types of problems as it helps people deal better with their particular situation. Participation and courage is important on the part of the individual and therapists are committed and supportive until a general sense of wellbeing develops.

**Hypnotherapy**

Hypnosis helps in overcoming some problematic issues as it can rehabilitate the way the brain reacts to triggers. It acts through the connection between the subconscious and the conscious mind. For example, anxiety can be triggered to high levels in some people when in a crowd, a dark room, crossing a bridge, when near water or during a public speech or simply when interacting with other people. Hypnosis seeks to uncover the source of a particular issue through a mental trance.

Webed (2016) defines hypnosis as using "guided relaxation, intense concentration, and focused attention to achieve a heightened state of awareness that is sometimes called a trance. The person's attention is so focused while in this state that anything going on around the person is temporarily blocked out or ignored. In this state, a person may focus his or her attention -- with the help of a trained therapist -- on specific thoughts or tasks".

Hypnosis, also can help someone to quit smoking or someone who does frequent movement such as nail biting. It helps with grief, anxiety, stress, motivation, fear, sleep disorders, depression and phobias.

Kat Martell (2016) explains that "in medicine and health psychology, hypnosis is used to treat irritable bowel syndrome, and reduce pain and discomfort associated with medical procedures such as childbirth, treatment of burns, and surgery where anesthesia cannot be used effectively".

Hypnosis is often use in psychotherapy, in many medical and psychiatric. The treatment is often used in chronic pain as well as psychosomatic problems. The therapist may ask you some questions just to know you better. It is important to feel at ease towards any question possible. Also one can suggest what is best for you. Basically, the first session can be longer than the second and third sessions. The therapist may dig very deep in feelings and answers provided by the patient under his care. The number of sessions needed before healing will depend on the person who is being treated with hypnosis. Healing depends on the ability of the therapist as much as on the response of the patient, on his state of health and on the nature of his problem. There are reasons to believe hypnotherapy is highly effective, sometimes more so and faster than other therapies; it can be used to treat many different illnesses.

Hypnotherapy may benefit people in other ways. It might help one to find new skills, feel more positive, live with new hopes and improve self-image. It might also help an individual to learn more about themselves and other people, it may help in acquiring new skills and insight. With time, one will be able to think more rationally and resolve problems with more ease.

## Interpersonal therapy

The Wikipedia website states that "interpersonal psychotherapy (IPT) is a brief, present-focused psychotherapy that centers on resolving interpersonal problems and decreasing symptoms. It is a highly structured and time-limited approach that follows a manual and is intended to be completed within 12–16 weeks" (2016).

This therapy actually focus on depression. The IPT was developed by Gerald Klerman and Myrna Weissman. By 1970, they studied depression and later it was adapted for other mental disorders. This therapy is still used by some therapists. The treatment is used by therapist, basically, those of who has Bipolar disorder, eating disorder, mood disorder, anxiety disorder, post- partum depression, bulimia nervosa, major depressive disorder and focus also for family therapy. Interpersonal psychotherapy has been proven to be effective treatment and many psychiatric residences in USA use this therapy to help patients and clients. The long term goal for this treatment is to find adjustment as a resolve to feel better with depression and other illness.

There are various things to consider when describing depression and interpersonal psychotherapy. A few examples are: what are the symptoms that effect from functioning. Second, how one is dealing with his or her personality, is there any issue related, and thirdly, how one is functioning socially. IPT short term treatment can last from 3 months to 4 months. During the therapy the therapist will identify the situation and find solution for better treatment. When being with the therapist, the client or patient has to realize the benefit of the therapy by experiencing the benefit. The therapist works collaboratively with the patient or client.

Usually, between a husband and wife there are interpersonal conflicts and disputes caused by social, family, school or work situations. The conflicts occur because of these various situations as well as expectations that are not met by the other. The difficulty in handling these problems may exacerbate marital problems and raise the stress level of the couple.

Grief is also another cause for not feeling good about oneself. Losing someone can be very depressing and hard to accept. Death is very dark in our mind, and some may not know how to deal with darkness, therefore it is important to be very open with the therapist so that he or she can help you better cope with sorrow.

When a dispute occurs between husband and wife, the role of the therapist is to guide them to better understand their mistakes and their strengths. The main goal of the therapist is to clarify misunderstandings. Each one must take charge for his or her life, which doesn't exclude the fact that sometimes, one takes the lead and the other one follows. Hence, the need to make changes in life to better function with one's loved one. The therapist usually enquires about the patient's past or present relationship with their partners. The therapist will provide support, help and guidance as he listens attentively throughout the process in order to bring greater clarity in the situation. He may actively participate in role playing in order to promote a better standpoint in regard to the advantages or the disadvantages of a situation. He or she will also do a communication analysis by letting the patient talk, with the intent to let go of the unpleasant and unwanted feeling and emotion from your mind and heart, all this in a therapeutic environment. The patient can also participate in a group therapy. This will help one to be freer in his or her environment, and members of a group can also learn by observing each other's behaviors. This requires channeling the participants' intentions toward a similar goal in regard to their common situation. By sharing their experiences, participants help each other. This shoulder to shoulder mutually supportive approach increases individual's motivation for a change for the better. When we chose to change, we chose to change first our self and then our environment. We can change our surrounding by changing our minds and feelings. There is hope for a better future by forgetting the past and controlling the present moment.

## Jungian psychotherapy

According to the famous Swiss psychologist, Carl Jung, imagination, fantasy, dreams and meditation are brought up into the present through narrative or action by using the unconscious mind. He called this active imagination. Carl Jung use analytical psychology to understand his concept of individuation. Basically, people develop through their emotional experiences. People integrate their negative and positive experiences and feelings. Jung coined the term *collective unconscious* to describe the phenomena of unconscious behaviors exhibited in every human nervous system. The collective unconscious portrays a mental image that cannot be explained historically. On the other hand, in Jung's theory of logos, it symbolizes philosophical theories that have connection with facts and reason. He often uses it to distinguish conscious versus unconscious. Nekia is used to describe a dark journey in a dangerous place. Jung defines Depth Psychology by using a method for discovering mental problems to treat them. Therapists deal with clients or patients to understand the source of the issue. To uncover the unconscious motives, Jung uses the archetypal psychology which was founded in archeology and anthropology. For many years, Carl Jung has worked with Sigmund Freud, but later each went into their own direction. Both are well known and people still use their theory and knowledge. Many scholars later developed the field of psychology.

## Logo therapy

Dr. Viktor Emil Frankl (1905-1997), a Viennese psychiatrist and neurologist, developed Logo therapy, which is a form of existential analysis. Logo therapy developed in and through Frankl's personal experience in the Theresienstadt Nazi concentration camp. He was devoted to understand the meaning of reality of human life. He has written at least 30 books and the most famous one is *Man's Search for Meaning*. When being in the camp, he realized that people who were around him and did not lost their sense of purpose and meaning of life were found to be able to survive longer than others.

Frankl's approach is based on the philosophical and psychological concepts.

1.  Freedom of Will
2.  Will to Meaning
3.  Meaning in Life

Logotherapy is used basically for extreme suffering, depression and painful situations. Frankl focus on the meaningful of life. Searching for the purpose to live and face various obstacles. Every life has a purpose and meaning to each individual, more precisely, finding the right meaning is the main goal. Hence, people can then see through their own fear, sadness, and suffering.

Dr. Frankl believed that there are three components of life. The human being is an entity consisting of:

1.  Body (soma)
2.  Mind (psyche)
3.  Spirit (noetic core)

According to Dr. Frankl, the following information is the attributes of the noetic dimension:

1.  Responsibility (not from, but responsibility to)
2.  Authenticity and creativity
3.  Choices
4.  Values

5. Self-transcendence
6. Will to meaning
7. Love
8. Conscience
9. Ideals and ideas

One may wonder how can one find meaning in life? According to Dr. Frankl, there are three ways of seeing life, more precisely, called the "meaning triangle".

1. Creativity
2. Experiencing
3. Change of attitude

The creativity can be explained through self-expression; one may have talent that can be seen in various ways. Experiencing can simply be living his or her life. For example, dealing with different types of relationship, live in various cultures, see nature differently, interactions with others. On the other hand, change of attitude is first to find the true meaning of life by reducing or removing suffering. There is a saying, "live your life", which basically means, do what you want and what you desire to do.

To end with logo therapy, Dr. Frankl's philosophy of life is simple: follow your regular life and routine. Everyday is a new day, what you learn from past, use it in the present, and what you learn in the present use it in the future. Dr. Frankl logo therapy is used mostly now by business managers, some ministers, counselors and educators and vastly used by people from every backgrounds such as colleagues, friends and family. What and how you will use yourself in life will be shaped by the choices you make today. When we search for happiness we will find happiness. Everyday is a new day!

## Music Therapy

As soon as we are born, we are surrounded by a variety of different sounds; we hear our parents, the doctor, the nurses, and the equipment of a hospital room. We are surrounded by the sounds of those around us at birth and, later, we are surrounded by natural and environmental sounds. There are so many different types of sounds that we hear during our lifetime, and we have been surrounded by these sounds since the dawn of humanity.

There are even some sounds that we may not be consciously aware of in our daily lives. It is nearly impossible for some people to make note of every sound that is around them, but with the help of modern technology, we are able to use these sounds to heal people with various illnesses. "There is an abundance of research supporting the healing properties of sound, including ultrasound, infrared, and consciousness altering audible sound. Therapeutic ultrasound, in particular, is widely popular as a medical treatment for a variety of ailments, such as kidney stones, tumors, cancer, teeth cleaning, bone regeneration, liposuction, killing bacteria" (2017).

Through this use of sound, the process of music therapy was created. With a simple search in *Wikipedia*, you will gain access to an array of information regarding music therapy. In short, music therapy is a non-verbal approach that is used by a professional music therapist by using musical instruments in general. The professional has a degree in music and therapy with a Masters Degree. Most music therapists help ill people by the use of music to better treat physical, emotional, mental, social, aesthetic and spiritual. It helps patients and clients to better manage mentally or even physically and to help improve their health. Music therapy is often used in various place such as correctional facilities, cancer centers, medical hospitals, schools, drug recovery programs, psychiatric hospital and community centers. The therapy works in two different ways; first the therapist and the second the patients or clients. The therapist uses many different musical instruments, or even writes and sings songs. Whereas, the patients or the clients participate by singing or even playing musical instruments. By doing this, it helps the patients and the clients to be creative and expressive by the use of the instruments. Some prefer singing with the therapists. The second way is to observe the therapist playing music while the patients or the clients draw, meditate, listen or do others types of activities.

Recent research has discerned that oftentimes, music therapy can be effective and beneficial for people to improve heart rate, stimulate of the brain, even to manage anxiety and to develop learning skills. For those with Alzheimer's disease, patients may find music therapy highly beneficial. Who can benefit from music therapy? Anyone can benefit from music therapy, thought the most common groups in therapy are usually children, adolescents, adults and elderly who suffer from mental health or other types of illnesses that music therapy can benefit.

## Narrative Therapy

Narrative therapy is a form of psychotherapy that helps individuals to value skills and knowledge comfort whatever problems they face. It is an approach that lets people see their competencies, commitments, beliefs, values, skills and abilities. It has various types of dimensions of diversity including ability, sexual orientation, gender, race, and class. This helps people to understand different platforms of life and to realize that they are not the only ones experiencing a different journey. The narrative therapy is based on stories that are made up of events that are happening over time and according to a plot. Based on these stories, one is able to visualize other people's perspective son their future, histories, and life. With problems, therapists try to find solutions over time. It has therapeutic conversation which involve problem-saturated story by the use of skills, clues to knowledge and by listening to people story.

### Parent-child interaction therapy (PCIT)

Based on Good Therapy Organization, the research on PCIT may be helpful for: "Building positive parent-child interactions. Developing positive child-rearing strategies. Reducing the likelihood of child physical and verbal abuse . Reducing child behavior issues (anger, aggression, defiance, etc.). Increasing communication and interaction skills within the family" (2017). When interacting with their children, parents or caregivers have to play a special role. The parents and caregivers may learn different approaches to understanding their children's mental health, developmental disabilities, language issues, behavior problems, and emotional situations. This is the only way to better fathom their child's behaviors. Moreover, the more that the parents and the caregivers will learn about the children's conditions, the more they will be able to adjust with them. Basically, parents and caregivers will learn to understand behaviors from the therapists. The therapists are there to show them how to behave and deal with complex situations. The treatments for the young children are based on their emotional and behaviors disorders that emphasis on improving the quality between parents-children and caregivers-children interaction patterns. Mostly, therapists use various techniques to coach parents and caregivers by using different skills. By being with the therapists one will learn how to decide which skills to work on. Usually, the session can be between half-hour to a few hours depending the therapist and where the session is held. Following the therapy, research and statistic shows that it is significant to improve behaviors disorders at the age of preschool age children. Parents and caregivers are there to better interact with the children.

## Psycho-dynamic psychotherapy

According to Haggerty, J. "The theory supporting psychodynamic therapy originated in and is informed by psychoanalytic theory. There are four major schools of psychoanalytic theory, each of which has influenced psychodynamic therapy. The four schools are: Freudian, Ego Psychology, Object Relations, and Self Psychology" (2017). Psychodynamic psychotherapy focuses on unconscious processes as it is based on person's present behavior. The main focus is to underline the self-awareness and understanding on their past or present behavior. It is based on understanding the unresolved conflicts and symptoms that can occur within a dysfunctional relationship with the self and the surrounding world. The therapy requires at least 2 years' worth of sessions. The reason why it takes so long is that it it is necessary to fully understand the aspect of one's identity in order to begin analyzing the personality and the early stages of emotional development. The therapy has main three functions: to treat depression, cognitive behavioral therapy, and interpersonal therapy. Based on the therapy it helps to understand the processes or behavior. The main goal is to help clients or patients to become more alert about their unconscious feelings into consciousness. The main goal for the councilor is to see through the session with the client-patients by guiding them to the right path.

## Reality therapy

Reality therapy was developed by Dr. William Glasser, a psychologist. His approach was based on psychotherapy and counseling. According to Glasser, those people who behave in inappropriate ways do not need help to find a defense for their behavior. The therapy has existed since 1965, and is based on choice therapy and on a strong understanding of choice therapy. This therapy is considered a cognitive-behavior approach to therapy. It is important to let the clients-patients understand his or her behavior by being aware of change of his or her thought and actions. The main focus is to find solutions in problem-solving situation. It focuses on making the right decision by taking his or her action by controlling one actions of one's life.

## Relationship Counseling

Whether you are married, living together, single, gay, lesbian or straight there will always be room for Relationship Counseling. There is no age requirement in order to participate in Relationship Counseling; the main goal for Relationship Counseling is to support those who go through difficult times between couples or are thinking about being in a couple. Those couples who face difficult relationships are the ones that mostly require the counseling. Usually, the most common therapy is face-to-face counseling, however, with modern technology counselors can also perform the therapy by telephone, email or even a chatting service. Moreover, the counseling can be done either with couples or even alone. The session depends on the client-patients. The therapy is confidential and non-judgmental. Some private companies may offer private sessions with a psychologist in case they need extra support. The sessions usually last from half-hour to one hour depending on the person and the therapist. The main goal for the therapist is to help you decide and make the right decisions. Counseling can make you move forward and make you realize the effects of your own actions and the actions that you are facing from your partner. It can also better guide someone who is not in relationship to better make the right decision for the future or just to understand relationship. Couples who usually face problem are those who go through domestic violence, substance abuse, work-related problems, social problems, self-esteem, life crises, depression, grief, anxiety, anger management, but mostly family stress and mostly couple relationship problems. All of the actions above are related to Relationship Counseling.

## Sex therapy

When discussing Sex Therapists, people may have misconceptions and think right away that they will teach their clients how to make love or they will perform with them. Sometimes, patients go there, not because of sexual problems, but with other situations and problems that they face in real life. Therapists discover by talking to them or by analyzing them. To become a Sex Therapist, you need to have a degree in therapy but many doctors become Sex Therapists depending the country of origin. Therapists talk about communication difficulties, desire, discrepancies, and sexual incompatibility. With time, motivation, commitment, and patience, sexual problems can be overcome. However, some couples are embarrassed to discuss about their sexual problems to the therapist. The only way to resolve problems is to open up and discussed about it. Specialists in the area are there to help you. They are trained to assist you. Depending the situation, if the problem either is medical or psychological, or depending on how motivated you are, the sessions may last depending how you feel about it and how the therapy was successful to you. If the therapist cannot help you, they will do their best to make a recommendation for you to someone who can help you with your particular situation and condition. Most Sex Therapists cannot prescribe medication, but if a doctor is also trained to be your Sex Therapist he or she may prescribe medication. Sex Therapists are trained to discussed and help you with the following information on sexual pain, difficulties related to sexual trauma, body image trouble, question about sexual orientation, anxiety about sex, sexual shifts due to physical changes, general dissatisfaction with your sex life, arousal problems, orgasm difficulties, low or lack of sex drive erection or ejaculation difficulties. If you have these problems maybe it is time that you consult a Sex Therapist or even discuss this with your medical doctor.

## Social therapy

Everywhere you go you will find someone, male or female, it is inevitable. We live in groups; whether with our colleagues at our workplace, friends, strangers we meet on the streets, and our family members. However, in some cases we may have trouble adapting to social situations. We feel pain and may feeling isolated. How do you solve this? Social therapists are there to assist us in better evolving our social skills so that we can feel free to socialize within our groups and explore more intimate relationships by being supportive.

Everyday we have to make decisions, whether simple or complex. With the help of a social therapist, you will be able to deal with difficult and complex decisions. Through the participation of work together, you will learn to overcome issues such as your fears, creativity blocks, fear of failures, and form successes. Some may choose group therapy, in which a group of people sits together, or interacts via phone or text, to discuss a variety of situations, good and bag. Through this social discussion, the brain begins to develop in a more social sense, your mind begins to open up to new scenarios, and value criticism and new ideas. Participating in the therapy can bring you to have new solutions to old problems, helping you better find solutions and answers in dealing with relationships. Try to find the purpose of being surrounded of beautiful people.

In some cases, the following information is based on social context and those who may suffer from: Anxiety, Shyness, Emotional connectivity, Frustration, Sadness, Depression, Confidence, Self-consciousness. The goal of Social therapy is based on trying to find the benefits and enjoying the interaction. Helping children, youth, and adults to form better social interactions., and teaching them to learn various aspects of life by going through experiences with other people. "The psychological benefits of social therapy include: Enhancing relationships, Developing personality, Increasing creativity, Increasing productivity, Encouraging collaborative efforts, Encouraging learning by example, Increasing independence, Enhancing self-regulation and coping skills, Decreasing feelings of loneliness and isolation, Reducing stress and anxiety, Enhancing social skills, Encourages friendships" (2017). One way to better assist is by group simulation, reinforcing positively, being passive or active, better communication, trying to do modeling, and to give back feedback to others. If ever you need to find resources or help, you may go to rehabilitation centers, specialized offices, hospitals, metal health facilities, school, or even the psychologist's office. There are enough resources and places where you can get help or guidance, so use it to your advantage.

It is great to be in couple and find love and the desire to live forever. However, more and more in the modern age, the marriage rate is declining and more and more couples are divorcing. There are too may changes that are happening in our society; some lose jobs and feel financial pressure, others have physical changes, some have psychological issues, for others educational levels may be of issue, while others have cultural and religion reasons, and a certain couples may even cite other factors. The statistics show that almost 50% of marriages end in divorce. When going through divorce, couples face various negative stages. Some go through difficult experiences such as denial, anger, guilt, blame, feelings of abandonment and feeling mostly disorganized. As a result, both parents and their children face suffering in the face of divorce. When deciding on divorce, most couples are uncertain about their future unless they have found another partner. While suffering, some may leave relationships for good and reasonable reasons even the choice was very hard and delicate. When couples face problems or issues some wonder if they need to take couples counseling. The following is information on why couples may fail in marriage.

First of all, communication has a big impact in a relationship. If both partners frequently bad mouth each other, disregard, insult each other, or put unnecessary pressure on their partners for anything, waste money for no reason, or hurt each other then there will be a negative gap and bad atmosphere when being in couple. As a result, this will lead to hurt feelings and a lack of trust and mutual respect.

Second, couples should be seen as a couple and not roommates. This will create a gap of communication. Not having conversations and intimacy can destroy a relationship quickly. The whole point is to let each other know that they are there for each other. Instead of isolating one another, they should open up. They should feel that they co-exist. Sometimes, however, it is important to let your partner having his or her own space, because we all need to feel free even though we care for and are committed to our partner for life.

Third, let your partner resolve their differences. Many may experience different things at time, but this should not stop you in finding a solution to fix a conflict. The best way to resolve something is to talk about it. Let your heart be free and open. Discuss what you feel and what you have in mind. If you need support, then consider having a third party involved. This can be a therapist, your parents, siblings, friends or someone else who can guide you to the right path and the right direction.

Fourth, when you see that your partner sees you from bottom of their heart negatively, you should ask questions. If they feel that everything you do is negative, that you don't want take care of her, or believes that you are planning a trap him or her. Your husband or wife feel that you are unfaithful, that you want to harm him or her, or that you are doing things behind her or his back. This may be frustrating if you want to show appreciation to your partner but he or she believes that you want to degrade him or her. Hence, with all types of negative behaviors you have nowhere to go to seek help. Use positive reinforcement, show that you really care and love him or her. If your partner screams at you, let him or her empty their thoughts and energy and take a full breath and tell one that you will be happy to discuss the situation. Make one feel loved.

Fifth, when you see that the conflict that you had would possibly serve to end the relationship you should put a big stop sign in front of you. When you continue arguing and disagreeing take a break - it might help you. Sometimes taking a back step helps to better heal and gives you more time to yourself. You can juggle your time, feelings, attention, and emotions Instead reinforce the thought that space and time are helpful. Returning from an absence can be beneficial. It can help couples to move on and forget the hurtful past.

Children tend to be the main factors in why a couple may choose to remain together rather than seek a divorce. Couples may feel that the best solution is to stay together in order to please their children, but in reality this sense of repressed conflict may damage children even more than a divorce would. However, in many cases having children can be a positive aspect in a couple's life, and some couples may feel that it is wise to remain together for the sake of the children. It is important to make a decision that you feel is right as long as it does not put your health in danger. If you are healthy and stable, you will be able to provide a better life for your children, whereas if you are sick you will be unable to provide support to your family unity. Children can bring healthy relationships and bonds among each partner. Love your children and love your partner. If needed seek counseling or find alternative resources to help you past a nightmare situation.

CHAPTER **2**

# PSYCHOLOGICAL AND SEXUAL HARASSMENT AT WORK AND AT HOME

## Psychological Harassment at Work

In most cases when applying for a job, your qualifications, work experience, education level, career goals, work ethic, values and attitude towards your coworkers, superiors and clients are all evaluated. The following paragraphs will focus on the job application process. This will lead you to be a better candidate for the position you are applying for. When it comes to your qualifications, you will need to open up and talk about yourself in order to demonstrate that you are fit for the job.

The essential is to focus on your work experience, your qualifications, your attitude, your qualities, and your intra- and interpersonal skills that are advantageous in the line of work you are applying for. Don't forget to mention why you are applying for the position, as well as what your goals and aspirations with this company are. It is important that you address every aspect of the job you are applying for.

When it comes to your attitude towards the job, mention that you would like to be fully involved in the job that you will perform. An interviewer may also ask you why you have chosen to quit your previous occupation and why you are so interested in having the job. This is when it is important to tell the truth about yourself. Some employers may prefer to hear your strengths, while others focus on your weaknesses. It is really important in interviews to be as honest as possible and not to hide anything. Refrain from criticizing your ex-employers; the past is the past and you should look to the future for the betterment of your career.

In terms of your values, focus on all your main strengths: what is most important to you? Some employers like to have an idea of the types of employers that you function best with to ensure a good fit. In this case, be positive yet honest and focus on the need for fairness and equality in the workplace. At work it is essential to get along with others. Tell the interviewer how much you value having good relations with your colleagues and supervisors. To achieve this, it is necessary to have good reactions when being criticized or corrected by a superior. Appreciate comments from people as they might help you improve in what you are doing. Usually, your employer does not only look at how you qualify for the job but also if you will get along with others. Your positive attitude will attract a better response from the working environment. When people accept you and you accept them, there is a bonding that leads to a productive work environment.

The end of the interview usually revolves around technical details such as salary. At this point, ask yourself make sure you have an idea of the salary and working conditions that you are looking for and what you are willing to accept from your future company. In some cases, the salary is already predetermined before you even apply for a job. If you intend on negotiating a salary, remain reasonable. Some choose to negotiate their salary before they start working. Other employers prefer to wait until new candidates perform well in order to discuss salary. At the end of interview, it is really important to ask questions, and it is also the time when future employers ask more personal questions. However, you may be asked some discriminatory questions, for example, if you take drugs or drink alcohol, or even how many times you were absent at work in your previous occupation. You may be asked if you have a criminal record, or if you had any arguments with your previous employers or employees. It is really important to stay calm when being asked these types of questions. Do not ruin your chance to get the job by telling lies or by blurting out useless information. Be reasonable and answer the questions in a way that avoid discrimination and awkwardness. For example, should one ask you if you miss work often, respond in a way that does not affect your reputation or the chance of getting the job. By being yourself you will get the job that you are looking for, and even if you do not get it on the first try, remember that there will be other opportunities to find the one that is suitable for you. There will be jobs you qualify for, others not, but do not get discouraged.

If you do not get the position you applied for, you should ask yourself why. There are various reasons for why one might not qualify for a job. If you were called for an interview, it is because the employers were interested in meeting you and perhaps in having you as a part of their team. Employers are willing to give a chance to those who show interest in their organization or company. More importantly, they need to see if you can compete with others and if you are suitable for the position. Some may even demand that you have experience in a certain field. All candidates have something they can offer in a given area of work. Some may get a job on their first try, others need more interviews to learn from their mistakes or to find the right place for them. If you do not find a job right away, use the help of organizations in your community. The Canadian and Quebec governments have various programs to aid people in their hunt for a job. You need to start somewhere in order to get where you want to be and achieve want you want.

The following lists fifty variables that may lead to poor performance in interviews. Review these to ensure that your first impression is a good one and to increase your chances in finding a job that is right for you.

1. Unkempt appearance
2. Arrogance
3. Aggressive behavior
4. Bad attitude
5. Difficulty to speak clearly
6. Weak voice
7. Poor vocabulary
8. Lack of a distinct career plan
9. Lack of ambition
10. Lack of work ethic
11. Apparent nervousness
12. Lack of participation
13. Lack of motivation
14. Poor academic performance
15. Unwillingness to accept minimal pay
16. Unwillingness to accept proposed job
17. Lack of maturity

18. Lack of respect
19. Lack of enthusiasm
20. Lack of knowledge of the field
21. Lack of experience
22. Lack of experience
23. Lack of tolerance to others
24. Poor social etiquette
25. Lack of respect to past employers.
26. Lack of respect of company policies
27. Lack of effort in learning the trade
28. Dishonest personality
29. Distant personality
30. Undecided personality
31. Marital problems
32. Family problems
33. Avoidance of questions
34. Jobs do not suit personal qualifications
35. Differing scheduling needs
36. Lack of autonomy
37. Lack of vision for the company
38. Lack of flexibility
39. Cynical personality
40. Lazy disposition
41. Lack of interest
42. Poor financial skills
43. Lack of achievements
44. Poor reactions to constructive criticism
45. Lack of punctuality
46. Lack of desire to question
47. Lack of desire to learn
48. Lack of initiative
49. Impolite disposition
50. Poor attendance

These fifty variables are not the only possible reasons why you may not have excelled in the interview. You may also have failed to answer the questions in the way your interviewer wanted. In some cases, employers ask that you complete a questionnaire in order to place you in a certain category. It helps them understand the type of person you are and aids in the selection process. There is typically no good or bad answer; employers are looking for the most powerful answer, the one that stands out to them. Each individual is different; therefore, answers and corresponding responses vary.

Here is a list of questions that are most often asked by interviewers in various fields. Most of these questions have many answers. There are no right or wrong questions or answers.

Questions
1. What does psychological harassment mean to you?
2. Why did you quit your previous line of employment?
3. What is your age?
4. Do you live alone or with someone?
5. What is your favorite sport?
6. Do you have any work restrictions?
7. Can you keep a secret?
8. What does mean confidentiality to you?
9. What is your opinion of men?
10. What is your opinion of women?
11. What is your opinion of children?
12. Are your working hours flexible?
13. How important is honesty in the workplace to you?
14. According to you, does religion have a place in the work environment?
15. What do you think of unionization?
16. Have you had previous misunderstandings with your colleagues or supervisors?
17. Have you previously gotten upset when talking with customers? Why?
18. What makes you feel most comfortable at work?
19. Do you accept constructive criticism by persons younger than you?
20. Do you accept constructive criticism by persons older than you?
21. How many jobs have you applied to before this one?
22. What are your plans for your future in this company?
23. Are there any skills you are seeking to develop at work?
24. What did you learn from your previous work?
25. Can we contact your ex-employers?
26. How would your previous employers define you if we contacted them?

27. What would your co-workers tell us about you?
28. What would your supervisors tell us about you?
29. When should work rules be applied?
30. Would you share company information with others?
31. How did you get your previous job?
32. Why did you leave your previous job?
33. Are you available 24/7?
34. Are you available on weekends?
35. Are you available during the daytime?
36. Are you available for the night shift?
37. Are you available on call?
38. What do you know about our company?
39. If you were to promote our company, what would you say?
40. Are you involved in any sport that would require you to be away?
41. Do you play a musical instrument?
42. Do you consider yourself a leader?
43. Do you consider yourself a team player?
44. Do you enjoy keeping a routine?
45. Do you like change?
46. Do you enjoy a flexible schedule?
47. What would you qualify as your biggest weakness?
48. Are you willing to travel for work?
49. Do you prefer to work alone or as part of a team?
50. Are you willing to be paid minimum wage?
51. What type of pay do you prefer: hourly, weekly, biweekly, or annually?
52. Do you like to work for commission?
53. Do you want bonuses?
54. If you job is terminated would you seek a severance package?
55. By what means of transport do you most often travel?
56. Which position in the company are you most interested in?
57. Are you open to working overtime occasionally?
58. Do you have any heath concerns we should be aware of?
59. Do you have any children?
60. Are you single?
61. Are you married?
62. Are you divorced?
63. Do you prefer to work on any particular days?
64. Have you ever lied to your boss?

65. Have you ever filed for bankruptcy?
66. Are you a morning person?
67. Are you willing to work overnight?
68. Did you win any contest?
69. What is your typical demeanor when approaching a client?
70. How would you sell something to a client?
71. Do you consider yourself a leader?
72. Are you a smoker?
73. Do you drink alcohol?
74. Have you ever taken or do you take drugs?
75. Do you take any medication we should be aware of?
76. Do you have any religious affiliation?
77. Do you have any political affiliation?
78. Do you prefer quality over quantity or vice versa?
79. How often do you require vacation?
80. How many days did you absent yourself from your previous job?
81. Do you aspire to have my position?
82. Have you ever had a burnout?

## How to Cope with Sexual Harassment at Work

It is not always easy to realize that you are being harassed at work by people that you respect or admire. It often comes as a shock. Suddenly, insecurities regarding the quality of your work come into play. All at once, it seems that you no longer fit in. Your colleagues may talk about you for no apparent reason. Some may make fun of you or even laugh at you. The following describes some methods to help you handle social stress in your working environment.

If you think you are being harassed, you should seek immediate help. Find support from someone inside the workplace whom you can trust or someone outside of work who can guide and support you. Sometimes, help can come in the form of a co-worker or a union representative, or, in many cases, your boss. A good place to begin is to start writing down everything that happens at work. Make sure to include who says what, and what is detrimental to you. Mention how you think the situation could be improved. It is important to gather as much information as possible in order to have a solid case.

The first step is to identify the principal element or cause for harassment. At first, you may want to verbally express your situation to someone you can trust and who can help solve the issue. If the situation gets worse, opt for filing a complaint. Make sure the issue is solely work-related. Ensure that personal problems are not causing the issue in the work place. If your issues stem from psychological, physiological, or physical issues, make sure to seek help from a counsellor, doctor, psychologist or psychiatrist. It can happen that personal problems are projected onto others in the work place, thus leading to the impression of discontentment in the professional environment. Emotional imbalances due to personal loss or mental illness can lead to a radical change in one's work behavior. Therefore, it is important to ensure that this is not your case before you take the next steps in solving work-related issues. Not all people have the same tolerance to extra stress or the same level of patience when it comes to dealing with problem situations at work, and may act out of character. This is normal, but the most important to remember is that physical violence is prohibited under all circumstances. Our society shows zero tolerance when it comes to physical violence. In certain situations, one may simply not know what to do or how to behave when faced with various challenges. Often, harassment comes as a complete surprise to many victims. Just keep in mind that freedom of speech is your right in Quebec and Canada. As such, do not remain silent when confronted with psychological harassment. Stand up for yourself, stand up for your rights. That being said, you should try not to act in any way differently with others should you be subject to harassment. Even when approaching the person who is causing you harm, remain respectful as much as possible; show that you are willing to find a solution to the problem. Try to discuss your problem with your employer and supervisors.

## Finding Help

- Talk to your employer
- Talk to your supervisors
- Talk to a work inspector
- Talk to a lawyer
- Talk to a doctor
- Talk to a psychologist
- Talk to a psychiatrist

- Talk to a counsellor
- Take time off if needed
- Discuss the issue with the human resources department at your work

## Other Tips

- Do not fear losing your job
- Be kind with yourself and others
- Be respectful towards others
- Be yourself
- Remain respectful
- Take the problem seriously
- Remain open to others in the face of adversity

## Defining the 'Ideal Job'

It is fair to say that every working individual seeks to have a steady job, ideal for them. The common ideal in Canada is typically full-time employment, either divided into 4, or 5 days a week, for a total of 40 hours weekly. A full-time job also includes 35 hours, 37.5 hours or even 40 hours weekly in Quebec, Canada. Full-time status varies depending on the employer and the hiring body, as well as the country. Other possible positions include part time, on call, seasonal or temporary work. In an ideal world, employees want to have the power to modify their schedule when necessary. This is only possible in particular working environments. In some companies, employees can keep a tally of their working hours. This is handy when one must miss a weekday of work - they can complete the hours they missed by working longer days the rest of the week. Schedules can also be fixed or flexible. For example, some flexible schedules require that employees start at 8:00 AM one day and the next at 2:00 PM. Fixed schedules, on the other hand, always have the same start and end times.

Hiring bodies also vary in terms financial arrangements. Some companies allow for salary advances while others do not have the financial capacity to do this. Salary is very important for a job to be considered ideal for a person. Money makes people happy. Money can change lifestyles for better or for worse. Good pay breeds motivation to work and motivation leads to a job well done. Good pay, however, does not first come without hard work. Keep this in mind and be smart with your finances and the rest will fall into place.

Almost all companies offer their employees the possibility to work their way up and earn positions of higher status. Through hard work and loyalty, a minimum wage employee can quickly become an assistant manager, manager, director, or even CEO. These kind of results are not the only benefit of giving your best at work. When you truly invest yourself in the company, it makes the working environment that much better, and it also leads to self-fulfillment and true satisfaction. You can feel proud that you gave 100% at work and you know that people above you are satisfied with your job. Full-time employees work almost at least one third of the day and this at least 4 to 5 day weekly. If you devote yourself fully, and enjoy your work, you will not even notice this is the case.

This is because it feels amazing to be respected at work. Moreover, stability and confidence in the workplace benefits domestic life. For example, it provides assurance that the resources are in place to take life-changing risks such as buying a house or having (more) children. This kind of stability also diminishes stress about missing work for health or personal reasons.

## Finding Happiness in the Work Place

The first step towards finding happiness in the workplace is to ask yourself who and what make you happiest at work. Respecting company policy and working diligently is the best way to earn respect from your supervisors, and in turn, self-satisfaction. If you perform well at work and respect your co-workers, you will find contentment at work. A job well done merits praise, but a sloppy work ethic does not. This is the principle of positive reinforcement. When you go above and beyond the call of duty, not only will you feel great about yourself, but your superiors will notice and be grateful towards you.

Autonomy and initiative are crucial in the workplace. Though your employers are charged with ensuring that employees have all the necessary tools to complete their tasks efficiently, it is up to you to bring up any issue or lack of resources that is preventing you from doing the best job you can.

Achieving the highest quality of work is of course the priority for any boss. This is why ensuring that employees and supervisors form productive teams is essential. Therefore, supervisor and employee combinations may change from time to time. If you find yourself in this situation, do not assume that this means that your boss is unsatisfied with your work; rather, keep in mind that any change is made with optimal efficiency as its primary goal. In other words, it could be that different pairings could lead to more harmonious performance in general, and is not necessarily aimed directly at your work. That being said, individual feedback about the working team is essential in achieving this goal. That's why many bosses are willing to hear you out and provide you with answers to any questions you may have. Your superiors want you to feel important at work, because you are.

Happiness includes, but is not limited to, good relations with your higher-ups at work. An equally important aspect is your relationship with your colleagues. When they appreciate your presence at work they may invite you outside of work, leading to the formation of friendships. When you have good colleagues you will not feel isolated in the workplace. Co-workers also notice good work ethic and may mention that you excel at what you do. The quality of work you provide will lead to a better overall product and will improve your working environment.

The following survey was conducted by Shere Hite (2000) and cites some statistics relevant to the workplace. Results may vary depending on nationality, age, and country of residence. Both men and women were asked in equal proportion the following questions. Answers are anonymous.

1.  Do women like their jobs?
    66% of female respondents in executive positions answered yes
    53% of female respondents in secretarial and clerical work answered yes
    41% of female respondents in middle management answered yes
    83% of female respondents in professional fields (doctors, attorneys, professors) answered yes

2.  Do men like their jobs?
    75% of male respondents in executive positions answered yes
    22% of male respondents in secretarial and clerical positions answered yes
    31% of male respondents in managerial positions answered yes
    67% of male respondents in professional fields (doctors, attorneys, professors) answered yes

3. Why do female executives like their jobs?
   72% of respondents feel it is because of status, and a feeling of importance
   91% of respondents of respondents feel it is because of the challenge
   74% of respondents feel it is because of the interesting interactions with people
   82% of respondents feel it is because of monetary benefits

4. Why do male executives like their jobs?
   73% of respondents feel it is because of status, feeling of importance
   69% of respondents feel it is because of the challenge
   66% of respondents feel it is because of the interesting interactions with people
   90% of respondents feel it is because of monetary benefits

5. Do women in middle management believe they can progress to become a member of the board of directors, an executive or a CEO?
   41% of respondents answered yes, through hard work
   22% of respondents answered no, because men hold all the higher-paying jobs
   37% of respondents do not want to progress in the corporation

6. Do men in middle management believe they can progress upwards?
   59% of respondents answered yes, through hard work
   23% of respondents answered no, there are others who are more favored
   18% of respondents do not want to progress in the corporation

7. Do men like working with women?
   31% of respondents answered yes, it lends to a better working atmosphere
   17% of respondents answered yes, if the women are not aggressive
   52% of respondents answered no.

8. Do women like working with men?
   41% answered yes, it makes work more interesting
   45% answered yes, if the men are equally hardworking
   14% of respondents answered no

9. Do you feel appreciated and paid fairly at work?

Men
31% of respondents answered yes
68% of respondents answered no

Women
44% of respondents answered yes
56% of respondents answered no

10. Have you experienced sexual harassment at work; i.e. been pressured sexually in a situation that could affect your job?

    Women:
    38% of respondents answered yes, seriously
    21% of respondents answered yes, slightly
    41% an of respondents answered yes, repeatedly

    Men:
    14% of respondents seriously
    68% of respondents slightly
    18% of respondents repeatedly

11. Do you believe that some slight separation between men and women at the office is acceptable?
    40% of female respondents answered yes
    65% of male respondents answered yes

12. In your opinion, should the CEO of the company where you work be married or single?
    33% of respondents believe CEOs should be in a stable marriage
    18% of respondents believe CEOs should be single, yet reasonable
    49% of respondents do not care about marital status of their employer or CEO

13. Have you ever been involved in a love affair at work?
    62% of female respondents answered yes
    71% of male respondents answered yes

14. If so, was it a positive or negative experience?

Men:

61% of respondents answered that it was a positive experience

30% of respondents answered that it was a negative experience

Women:

27% of respondents answered that it was a positive experience

73% of respondents answered that it was a negative experience

15. In your opinion, do men bully other men more than other women?

Men:

23% of respondents answered that women are bullied more than men

77% of respondents answered that men are bullied more than women

Women:

81% of respondents answered that women are bullied more than men

19% of respondents answered that men are bullied more than women

16. Based on your experience, do female employers treat female employees differently than male employees?

Men:

91% of respondents answered yes

9% of respondents answered no

Women:

94% of respondents answered yes

6% of respondents answered no

17. Does your wife, husband or partner act jealous, at times, of people with whom you work, particularly those of the opposite sex?

Men:

61% of respondents answered yes

25% of respondents answered no

32% of respondents answered yes, sometimes
64% of respondents answered that it depends on context

Women:
39% of respondents answered yes
62% of respondents answered no
31% of respondents answered yes, sometimes
43% of respondents answered that it depends on context

18. How would you feel if your corporation had a board of directors comprised only of women?
    13% of respondents answered that they would be alarmed
    16% of respondents answered that they would be pleased
    38% of respondents answered that they would feel worried
    18% of respondents answered that they would not like to work for such a corporation
    15% of respondents answered that they would like to work for such a corporation

## Defining sexual harassment

Sexual harassment in the workplace and in other professional or social contexts involves unwanted sexual advances or obscene remarks aimed at colleagues, most typically women.

Though women are most often the victims of sexual harassment, some men are also targeted. That being said, gender does not dictate how each individual reacts to harassment. Different people have different definitions of sexual harassment. One may consider the occasional sexually-driven comment to be harassment while another may only be set off once physical advances are made. Sexual harassment includes a wide array of verbal and non-verbal displays. Regardless of types of harassment, victims often feel affected emotionally after the fact. Psychological and emotional healing can take from many days to many years, depending on the seriousness and frequency of the incidents, and depending on the individual. Moreover, the physical violation can lead to a feeling of disgust and a sense of loss of dignity. For many, it is difficult to explain these feelings and the experience to others, which leads to a sense of isolation and distrust.

# Understanding the context of sexual harassment

*Characteristics of the workplace*

- o What is the size of the business?
- o What is its degree of economic stability?
- o To whom does it belong?
- o How many owners are there?
- o How many men and women work in this business? In this department?
- o Is there a turn-over of female personnel?

*Describing the situation*

- o Is the man/woman unionized? On probation?
- o Where is he/she situated in the hierarchy of the business?
- o How long has he/she been employed there?
- o Is he/she employed there?
- o How are her or his work relationships with her colleagues and with his or her superiors?

*Describing the harasser*

- o How long has he been working for the business?
- o Where is he situated in the hierarchy of the business?
- o Is he or her immediate superior?
- o Is he or she a member of the same union as the woman or man?
- o What type of relationship does he or she have and has he or she demonstrated with other employees?
- o In his position at work, how many women does he have contact with on a daily basis.

*Other factors to consider*

- o Are there any witnesses?
- o Are his/her colleagues aware of the situation?
- o Is the harasser harassing or has he harassed other men/women?
- o Has a doctor been consulted?

o    Has the quality of work provided by the victim diminished since the harassment began?

o    Up to what point does the man/woman depend on this job financially?

o    Does he/she have support at work and at home?

o    What can he/she do or undertake alone? With assistance?

## Defining psychological harassment at home

Psychological harassment is something terrible for anyone to bear. It is often characterized by repeated personal accusations directed at the victim, the instigation of arguments over matters that do not merit as much attention as they get, and the exaggeration of quarrels by bringing unrelated topics into the argument. Harassers tend to create excessive stress for reasons unknown. Often the offender twists the truth or even lies to emphasize his/her points. Accusations are likely accompanied by intimidating non-verbal behaviour, such as hitting, throwing, or breaking inanimate objects, and making excessive noise to instill fear in the victim. Insults and swearing can be combined by the offender to increase hurtfulness of the verbal assault. This can affect the victim's dignity and psychological integrity, and can cause psychological and emotional damage.

It also takes a toll on one's self-confidence. Psychological abuse can also be taken outside the household by the offender by spreading rumours or by publicly ridiculing the victim. In extreme cases, conversations may be recorded in order to emotionally blackmail the victim, or to prove a point. Threats and punishments of all kinds can also be made by the harasser to achieve his or her ultimate goal.

An aggressor will do many things to test your patience and character, just to see how you react in front of him/her or her or others. Harassers will find any and all ways to blame or punish their victims. A household example could be that one's significant other wants something in particular but one refuses to provide it. Subsequent verbal or physical abuse could ensue as a method of punishment.

Living in a household where one is being psychologically harassed is difficult, and can lead to a desire to leave. Abusive words and dramatic outbreaks as a means to get attention takes a toll on victims. It also destroys relationships and breeds disrespect. Relationships of this sort may not last for too long. Reactions of victims to harassment vary greatly. Some bear the burden longer than others. Different people have different limits and patience levels, and it is important to communicate these to one's aggressor in order to make a change.

Psychological harassment is a serious matter that can affect both the home and work environments. This is why it has to be treated with complete seriousness. Destructive atmospheres take the pleasure out of being at home or at work, depending on the case.

## Harassment in the workplace

Harassment in the workplace affects a person's psyche and has a direct consequence on their self-esteem and desire to work. Sometimes health issues even arise as a result of severe harassment.

In cases of harassment in the workplace, it is wise to approach your boss or the human resources department to explain your situation. They are responsible for helping you find a solution to your work-related problems, whether that involves simple advice or re-organizing your social environment.

Harassment can take on many forms, but is most commonly verbal. Verbal attacks in the workplace can damage one's sense of integrity and reputation. Attacks aimed at one's work ethic and performance can seriously affect one's confidence. Rumours spread by the aggressor regarding the victim can often even bring the victim's character into question by co-workers. There are multiple possibilities for what a rumour can consist of; some target the victims' loyalties or honesty, by insinuating, for example, that he/she has stolen from the company. In situations such as these, even if accusations are totally false, co-workers and superiors may begin to have doubts. It thus makes it difficult to convince them of one's loyalty and integrity, consequently leading to a disturbing working atmosphere.

It is difficult to understand exactly why an aggressor may decide to spread false rumours about their targeted victim. It may be that the person who is creating rumours does it as a way to elevate his- or herself in the workplace by lowering others. It could be a show of dominance and a way of proving why he/she is not compatible with the target in question. It could also be driven by a sense of competition, jealousy, or simply bad team spirit. Competitiveness can push one to manipulation, making it so that his/her competitor does not get a bonus, or at a lesser extent, so that the victim of harassment is not seen well in the eyes of their boss. In cases of competition-driven harassment, the harasser will do everything in his/her power for the victim not to rise above them in the workplace.

Of course, competitiveness and jealousy walk hand in hand. Jealousy is part of human nature and is normal to a certain extent. Only when jealousy impedes on performance and on working relations is it seen in a more negative light.

Harassment does not only happen between co-workers. It can also happen that a client will be very rude towards an employee. Swearing, yelling, and making a scene in general are common traits of a client harassing an employee. These incidents are humiliating and can harm employees emotionally. Often, workers may not know how to behave or what to say in the face of these attacks. In these cases, it is always best to refer customers to one's superiors.

# CHAPTER 3

# REACTING TO PSYCHOLOGICAL HARASSMENT

Body language is an essential tool in effective psychological harassment. Aggressive gestures are key features in arguments. These may include repetitively waving arms or legs, hitting the walls or table, and making angry gestures with the arms. Excessive noise is also a common way of enhancing the harasser's point. That being said, it can also happen that the attacker is not aware of their hostile body language, and may behave in this manner until someone mentions how unacceptable their behaviour is. For example, it is not respectful when one's boss yells at or loudly calls one out in front of their co-workers. What is the solution in this situation, one might ask? The best way to behave in this case is not to take it personally and appear unaffected. However, it is also a good idea to discuss the issue when a better time presents itself, when all parties are calmer.

Some harassers have less intimidating demeanors but are more abusive verbally. Examples of some very aggressive remarks include: "you look fat", "why is your face so ugly?", or "What's that smell? I think you did not clean your ass." Hearing these types of insults is very hard. It feels terrible when a stranger says something along these lines, but feels even worse when a partner, friend, or colleague says it. When someone makes this kind of brutal remark or comment, it is sometimes best not to reply in order to avoid a full-on argument. Usually, in order not to create more tension with this person, it is better to avoid any contact. Feign ignorance. Refusing to grant the abuser attention is a form of victory.

There exist other types of psychological harassment, such as emotional blackmail. This type is most commonly carried out by someone relatively close to the victim. The aggressor threatens to spread lies or rumors to people who are important to the victim if he/she does not do what the harasser says. The abuser uses the fact that victims want to avoid certain secrets being known or losing face in front of people they care about to get what they want. The solution in a situation like this is tricky because it is very hurtful to hear such things or be threatened in such a way. It is especially hard to deal with when the people making the threats are friends, family, or co-workers.

Manipulation does not only come in the form of blackmail. Many people get very creative in terms of manipulation to get what they want. Whether manipulation is planned or not, manipulators use all sorts of words and actions to get their victims' attention; some are better than others. This kind of harassment can be difficult to spot because some of these people actually try to gain their victims' trust and friendship.

Harassment and manipulation are becoming easier to do and more destructive with the increase in household technologies. That said, these technologies can also be used as a means of protecting oneself against harassment. For instance, in recent years, more and more people are using recorders. These can be used to record conversations where one's superior or co-worker is being aggressive towards him/her. The recorded conversation serves as evidence of harassment, and is useful when backing one's claims.

Of course, people who record conversations could also be doing this with bad intentions, or because of psychological problems. These recorded conversations can be used for bad purposes, such as blackmailing.

One particular type of recording is the one used in call centers. All employees in call centers working at customer service understand that their calls may be recorded. This is normal. However, if these recordings are used to mock and ridicule one's performance, then this is considered harassment. The usual use for these recordings is for quality-assurance by your boss or supervisors. The purpose of listening to employees is not to punish but to help them. In other environments, such as banks, government institutions or private companies, recording conversation is a way of protection for the employers. It's like a self-defense mechanism and a way to improve overall performance within the company. Any use outside of this that harms employees or customers is harassment and unlawful.

The use of recording devices without prior consent in the home environment is a reason for alarm. If one's significant other records private conversations between the two, one should ask oneself the reason behind this. Is he/she using this as a defense mechanism or as a weapon? Is he/she recording loud and intense arguments to show the public the victim's bad side, to gain sympathizers? Recording in such a manner is treating the victim, in a sense, like a criminal. This is not good and not normal, and this relationship should be either fixed or terminated to prevent further pain. Another possible use of these recordings can be for self-analysis and understanding of personal behaviour when calm and when angered, or again to help their partner understand why their behaviour is unacceptable. It could be that the use of a tape recorder is for the benefit of the relationship.

Social media allows others to provoke their victims in simple ways like commenting on photos or on written posts. There are many reasons for criticism, like dislike of a photo one posted, or disagreement regarding a comment. Views differ greatly and disagreements arise from these. All sorts of web surfers from around the world can see each others' photos and videos. Many problems arise from this lack of privacy. For example, one may tell their employer something about themselves, but the opposite is portrayed on their online profile. Again, one may say they miss work for health reasons, but will actually be out socializing and this is published on their social media page. And of course, issues surrounding hacking into accounts and blackmailing owners are to be considered as well. Social networking sites can also be to blame for insecurities leading to broken relationships. Social networking has a good and bad side. One may find a partner through the use of social networking, another may lose friends. If one is being harassed on social media sites, they should refrain or limit their use.

With technology, everything seems to move fast. Having a phone at all times has become habit. People text while eating, cleaning, traveling by public transport; everyone texts all the time, whether it is inside or outside of the house. Horrifyingly enough, people even text and drive, resulting in the accidents and deaths of many. Now, cars are equipped with technologies to allow for hands-free communication whilst driving. Technology is constantly improving and changing radically. New technologies have changed our visions and ways of communicating. Sending messages to friends and family can influence their day - it can bring them happiness or sometimes discontentment. Texting acts as a screen between the sender and the receiver and can make some write whatever they want to family members, partners and friends. Writing has much power and impacts mental and emotional states. Some people may abuse this fact. Certain people may purposely write things to offend or irritate someone. Many couples communicate by text messaging a lot, and sometimes harsh wording can be cause for anxiety. Though all have the freedom to write whatever they want while texting, it is important to remain responsible for one's words at all times.

## Depression and its causes

Depression is common in people who go through psychological or sexual harassment at work or at home. When an individual is going through difficult times he or she may have low self-esteem, a sense of disorganization, and may be emotionally vulnerable. Extreme cases even go so far as to having suicidal thoughts. Other reactions may include pessimism and a negative outlook on life. This can affect people around them and lead them to also become negative and to lose patience quickly.

Periods between instances of harassment can be equally distressing as the event itself. The victim may suffer of agitation, nervousness, and impatience towards others. He or she may have trouble sleeping or feel fatigued. Irrational thoughts and difficulty concentrating are common ailments. Anxiety may become an issue that is increasingly difficult to handle. Some can even have problems with their memory. Some may hide the hurt from harassment longer than others, but eventually, be it after months or years, they can simply melt down or explode because they cannot take it any longer. However, some keep suffering until they realize they needs medical help. At that point, they need to seek help from a doctor, psychologist, psychiatrist or any other health specialist. Medical specialists can help victims find solutions and become emotionally balanced, psychologically stable, morally fit and physically pure you. This helps victims overcome their past and gain confidence.

## The most common reasons why one might begin seeking help from a counselor or therapist are:

In many cases, the most common problems occur between couples and partners who are facing a breakup or an upcoming divorce. Human emotion is too powerful during suffering, and not acknowledging your negative emotions may lead to clinical depression. In the case that clinical depression occurs, severe health issues may often take hold as a result. Losing a partner is a very difficult thing to manage, and suddenly becoming a single parent may also be painful. In some cases, sharing the custody of a child or children may become sorrowful, and expensive in the case of childcare payments. Unexpectedly, living alone can also become a difficult task, as raising children alone can become hectic.

Often, people realize the value of their partnership long after leaving their partner, while others begin to feel more positive emotionally or mentally, especially if they suffered emotional, mental, or physical abuse at the hands of their partner. Still others may suffer due to the loss of a job or for career reasons. Maintaining a certain standard of living for a few years, then suddenly having to change the way you survive due to the loss of a job may create severe financial issues between couples, family members, and even within oneself. Making less money can become difficult, and finding a new job to survive can be even harder.

Many people who suffer from this type of pain may find themselves in the midst of depression. This can take form in difficulties in every day tasks such as getting out of bed, going to work, or even simple tasks such as brushing one's teeth. Finding the energy to tackle simple situations becomes impossible, and they may eventually come to feel that life has no point, no color, and may begin to lose spirituality and faith. In many cases, an individual may find themselves unable to perform sexually, or unable to achieve pleasure during sex. This may be due to a lack of an intimate partner, or emotional turmoil. While there are many different types of treatments for depression – including medications and therapy – it is best to first tackle the situation as holistically as possible – that is, through therapy – before relying on medications that can result in negative side-effects. Many specialists may recommend better diet and increased exercise, socialization, therapy, self-discovery, volunteer work, developing new interests, and meeting positive like-minded people as beneficial methods of self-therapy.

Many individuals who suffer from negative situations may begin to develop anxiety, feeling hopeless or nervous, and having panic attacks. Phobias, such as a fear of public speaking, can also be a reason why one should consult a therapist or simply go to counseling. It is important to take this seriously as one may become very deranged, so the quicker you seek help, the better the chance of recovery.

This can also create anger. People may find themselves unable to cope with the stress of everyday life and find themselves exploding in anger. It seems that we often express our anger and are very mean and rude to those we love the most. We are angry because he or she did not do what were asked or simply could not cope with. It is important to learn healthier ways to communicate by expressing and coping with anger. Learning to express emotions in a healthy manner can be beneficial not only for themselves but also between friends and family.

Nowadays, it is estimated around 50% of couple go through divorce, especially in Western societies such as the UK and USA. Couples have difficult time with themselves or with raising their children. New parents find it challenging to raise their new step- children. Some are able to cope, while others become a nightmare. It may result in sibling rivalry, custody battles, and financial concerns. Some step-parents do not tolerate their partner's children. The father or the mother are in-between two families. Their children are confused as to who to call mother or father after going through a separation or divorce. Hence, involving family members in the therapy process is important in order to facilitate healing.

Many broken families are not aware of professional therapy. In this case, a professional advisor may help family members to attend therapy if they face problems. In some cases, their children become an issue. Some children are bullied in school, while others have different types of problems. Children also become anti-social and some spend large amounts of time texting, playing video games, watching uncommon things online such as porn, or staying home continually tweeting or spending time in online social gatherings. They forget that there is an outside world. There was a time where children used to go play outside and wanted to stay outside, but with the advancement of technology people or mostly children stay at home and spend time with their computers. Slowly they develop mental health problems. When children have problems in school some parents may become frustrated in their office or at work, which causes further problems with their surroundings.

Another problem that occurs in many families is addiction. Addictive behaviors may begin with an obsession. An individual may find themselves spending time and energy focusing on obtaining their substance of choice. Individuals who participate in substance abuse may act alone or even secretly. Others may practice substance abuse in a collective manner, with friends or even strangers in many cases. Some individuals may suffer through a stage of denial, or the refusal to acknowledge the fact that they have an issue with their addiction. In many instances, an addicted individual commonly feels the need to use drugs in order to handle their personal problems. However, substance abuse is merely a temporary relief from the realities of everyday. In other cases, an individual may feel that they are able to escape from their troubles through substance abuse.

The majority of individuals who suffer from substance abuse are addicted to drugs or alcohol. A large amount of people are addicted to smoking cigarettes or cigars. In many cases, the individual feels that they will feel physically or mentally better if they take drugs or drink alcohol. However, in cases when an individual takes large doses of alcohol, it is considered alcoholism. A person in this situation may drink large amounts of alcohol within a short period of time, as a way to escape from their reality by being drunk or high. Even more dangerously, individuals may operate a vehicle while drunk or high, causing a traffic accident that may result in more than one death. In this same vein, many individuals come to have issues with the law, being arrested due to their substance abuse. Without realizing what they are doing, an individual may also suffer financial difficulties due to their addiction to expensive substances, resulting in even more difficulties in their daily life. For example, an individual who smokes cigarettes will purchase a packet of twenty cigarettes, costing them $11. This results in a monthly cost of about $330, and a yearly cost of $3,960 on cigarettes alone. By quitting this addiction, an individual can save almost $4000 in a year, allowing them to save the money for more important endeavors, such as paying off debt or a mortgage.

Other individuals may find themselves behaving differently in front of their partner or their families as a result of their abuse. Statistically, males are found to take more drugs than females of the same background. This is due oftentimes to genetics and family history; when there is an ancestor who suffered from addiction in the past, later members of the family run a high risk of developing one themselves. Alcoholics, for example, are more likely to have a blood relative who is also dependent. For smokers, smoking cigarettes increases the risk of influencing family members to smoke, whether psychologically or through second-hand smoke addictions. Those who suffer from mental illness are at an increased risk of becoming addicted to nicotine, alcohol, and other drugs. It is always in your best interests to avoid harmful and addictive substances, and maintain a limit on recreational substances such as alcohol. After all, it is your life and your health that you are risking.

Eating disorders are another cause for physical and mental illness. Some individuals may struggle with their weight, and others may find that they are not eating simply because they do not find themselves having an appetite, oftentimes as a result of the stress of daily life. Women are the most commonly affected demographic of eating disorders; the desire to lose weight despite the reality of their physique may result in anorexia nervosa, bulimia, and other eating-related disorders. A specialized trainer may be of assistance in this case; information on how to keep in shape through healthy and safe methods will prevent eating disorders.

Another reason for attending counseling is having low, or a lack of, self-esteem. We are only human; we may sometimes not make the best impressions and can lack assertiveness, leading to isolation and unhealthy relationships. This can also affect performance in the work place. Through healthy coping mechanisms, one can learn to become more assertive and confident without becoming aggressive. Taking the initiative to seek out a counselor or therapist will allow you to discover the value of working with a mental health professional; once you have broken this boundary it becomes easier to understand the self.

Individuals who have attended therapy have appreciated the process and found it overall a useful investment. "According to Howes, R. PhD, Psychology Today's own 2004 survey, more than 27% of all adults (an estimated 59 million people) received mental health treatment in the two years prior. Of this group, "47% report a history of medication, but no therapy; more than a third (34%) report a history of both medication and therapy; and 19% report a history of therapy, but no medication." If my math is correct, that means somewhere around 30 million adults were in psychotherapy during that two year period (2014)". That is a significant number; some individuals pay for counseling while others receive free care due to their financial situations, health systems, or their country of residence. The sooner one attends therapy, the sooner one will begin to feel the positive effects of counseling. The main goal for doctors, psychologists, therapists or counselors is to help you develop a way to understand what is going on with you and your surroundings. Professionals are there to help you; therefore, you should not be afraid to seek help.

Communication is important in all relationships; many individuals utilize therapy as a way to assist them in becoming stronger communicators. When one cannot explain something to someone or is unable to understand what the other is saying, conflicts may arise. You will find many highly qualified therapists and counselors who are skilled at helping people communicate their feelings and resolve their issues.

What happens when one cannot trust their therapist, or simply does not have the financial capabilities to finance counseling? Depending on their issue, individuals may seek assistance from friends or family members, who can provide support, information, guidance, and experience. This level of communication and support may be enough for many; experience is the father of wisdom, and oftentimes older family members may be able to provide enough advice for an individual to work on solving their own issues. If, however, your family members are unavailable or you do not wish to burden them with your issues, you may choose to rely on a close friend instead.

Usually, when one is suffering from distress, side-effects may include the inability to sleep, eat, study, socialize, or otherwise enjoy life. If you suffer from any of these symptoms, it is advisable to seek medical assistance. Therapy may be your final option, as oftentimes issues may be medical in nature. Therapy can be seen as support in coping with grief, physical illness, the end of a relationship, career changes, or other life-altering events. It is important to allow yourself a chance to heal your body and mind, to be open minded and understanding of yourself. Through self-exploration, you may be able to determine your personal goals, career goals, relationship needs, and other life-enhancing areas.

## What is the solution for Psychological Harassment in the Workplace?

People often go through difficult times at home, at school, or outside, but it is difficult for many people to believe that they may suffer from psychological harassment in the workplace. One can understand that at home, your parents, siblings, or even your partner can become toxic, in many cases even your children, your friends or even strangers outside - but why would your coworkers do such things to create a negative atmosphere and put your emotions at stake. Why would your coworkers suddenly be working against you in a scenario where they are creating a drama to make your life miserable? Why are they doing everything to hurt your feelings? Why are they lying to fire you? Why are they bulling you?

You may have many questions but very few answers. Your coworkers that you talk with freely, that you laugh with openly, and eat with at the same table at your workplace, are suddenly creating rumors about you. You cannot understand why they are expressing such suddenly different behavior, why it is so repetitive, why they blame you or use brutal comments that hurt your feelings, why they act like that suddenly with you. They may say things to hurt you morally, psychologically, socially, and create an unwanted atmosphere so that people around them start disliking you. It becomes an environment that you may consider very intimidating, aggressive, or even abusive. As a reaction you may have hard time sleeping at home, your mood may become disturbed, you slowly start feeling ashamed of what you may hear about you. You may doubt that people are they just to give you hard time. Some may get discouraged and quit their job or even become depressed. A few percentages become deranged and suicidal. Over time those you trusted become your worst enemies and you become intolerable. Sometimes, you may wonder is it because of you are not white, or black, or brown or yellow or red? Why are you the targeted one?

What you should do is write down everything that happens at your workplace. Seek help if you feel it is needed. Talk to your doctor about it. Talk to a counselor or a psychologist. Use the company or government resources. Find out what your stressors are and try to change your negative thoughts. Harassment can be discriminating. Usually it is unwanted physical or verbal behavior that can offend or humiliate you. Someone that is harassing you oftentimes will do it repeatedly over time. Sometimes, one single offense can become serious harassment.

What are some possible things that your coworkers may think or say about you? They may criticize you on your job performance; either you are too slow or too fast on doing your work. They are never fully satisfied with what you do or tell them. They pinpoint everything that you do - it is never your way but it has to be done they way. Judge you based on your physical appearance. They accuse you of being a thief, even though you did not take anything from them or the company or from outside or even from your coworkers. Some enjoy putting the spotlight on you and degrading you as much as possible just because you do not agree with therm. They want you to lose face toward them and the society. So that people see on their eyes and you being dishonest and disrespectful. Sometimes unwanted behavior can come from supervisors, coworkers, customers and anyone that the victim interacts on the job. Furthermore, when being humiliating the work interference can be as sabotage by using verbal abuse. With new technology, one may harass you through the use of internet or even by calling you, saying negative things, or reading or hearing unwanted words. Defamatory libel can also occur when your boss talks bad about you to others or write down things about you.

## Here are some steps you should prepare when filing a complaint for psychological Harassment.

Write It Down: by keeping a detailed journal with what is creating harassment.

List witnesses: write as many names as possible, people who are willing to help you. If there are you witness write down, there names.

Your voice counts: Talk to someone you trust or someone who can help you in the present time and future time.

Get Help: Find someone who can help you such as your supervisor.

No need to get aggressive: Be calm as much as possible. Try not to react to the bullying or harassing by being quite.

Contact company or Government resources: a company advisor, it could be a mediator, human resources advisor, someone who is responsible for employee assistance.

Non-profitable organizations or associations: someone who can help you outside from work if you do not trust people from work.

Find out what causes the workplace stressors: what triggers you or what stress you. Find a coping mechanisms.

Find a way to change your negative thoughts: Try to learn and identify what cause you negative thoughts and change direction. Everybody can change negative thoughts and replace it by positive thoughts. It is a matter to try it.

Writing a journal: always best to write what is happening, we tend to forget many things due to continue information in our mind and brain but continue to be hurt because of what is happening to us. By writing it you can use it also in the future and who knows you may write a book.

Find ways to relax. You will have many things in your mind and you brain. Main things is to be able to control your mind. Try to forget bad memory and replace it with good one.

You should keep a record. Seek advice. Check for a workplace bullying policy. Also use counseling service. By doing this you might be in good hands. By keeping a record, you will have better voice. Seeking for advice will help you to pass over harassment. By knowing the policy, you will be better in control. You will know your rights. Never refuse to receive help. There is various way to get help and one way is through counseling service.

## Reporting Harassment

If you are not the victim of harassment, be kind with the victim. If you find yourself in the position of witness to harassment, reach out and help the victim. Often we become victims without knowing why we suffer and have pain emotionally, psychologically we are deranged, physically we are abused, and some may even suffer sexual harassment. It is important that you report to the human resource departments of your company especially when your colleague is in danger or feels uncomfortable to express his or her situation. You tried everything to resolve the problems or situation but you do not arrive to a conclusion, hence maybe the best solution is to contact you superior or even employee from the HR department. Remember - the sooner you choose to take action, the better you will resolve. When filling the complain of harassment, one will launch an investigation. Often, disciplinary action or even termination can occur. Usually this can happen with evidence against the harasser. Complaints can come in the form of written on a paper, telling on the phone, by person; explaining the situation or even with modern technology by email or texting or even by fax. Sometimes, the victim may not wish the harasser to know or to take action but he or she may ask to put a not on his or her file. Like this, one will be able to guide the victim better. Often until the investigation is not complete the management direction cannot take action, therefore, you need to be patients.

# Workplace Bullying

Usually, someone who is going through bulling is living a very emotional and shameful life. He or she is surrounded with workers or group of people who are saying or doing an action repetitively, for no reason, with inappropriate behaviors. This can provoke an unhealthy or unsafe situation at workplace. Coworkers may use direct or indirect verbal abuse or physical violence by hurting one. Verbal abuse can be by threatening with an aggressive way, spreading rumors, insulting, provoking, screaming or even lying to one. Some people use intimidation to hurt an individual. Bullying can also be by telephone, messages, emails, texts, fax or even letters.

Bullying can begin due to cultural conflict, religious beliefs, genders, sexual orientation, education, and most commonly race. Conflicts start by not having the same opinion, beliefs, disliking something, not respecting other people value. When there is a negative treatment which can be seen unreasonable or offensive we can justify that there is bullying at play.

In the Positive Solutions there are two main types of bullying behavior, overt and covert. Here are the following example how one can be bullied.

"Examples of overt, or obvious, bullying include:

- abusive, insulting or offensive language;
- behavior or language that frightens, humiliates, belittles or degrades, including criticism that is delivered with yelling and screaming;
- inappropriate comments about a person's appearance, lifestyle, or their family;
- teasing or regularly making someone the brunt of pranks or practical jokes;
- interfering with a person's personal effects or work equipment;
- harmful or offensive initiation practices; and
- physical assault or threats. Covert or more subtle behavior that undermines, treats less favorably or dis-empowers others is also bullying, for example:
- unreasonably overloading a person with work;
- setting timelines that are difficult to achieve or constantly changing deadlines;
- setting tasks that are beyond a person's skill level;
- ignoring or isolating a person;

- deliberately denying access to information, consultation or resources; or
- unfair treatment in relation to accessing entitlements such as leave or training (2017)."

"What are the possible effects of bullying?

The costs to an organization may include reduced efficiency, unsafe work environment, increased absenteeism, poor morale, increased workers' compensation claims or civil action.

The reactions of individual workers will vary according to the nature of the bullying. It is possible that workers who are bullied will experience some of the following effects:

- stress, anxiety, sleep disturbance;
- panic attacks or impaired ability to make decisions;
- incapacity to work, concentration problems, loss of self-confidence and reduced output and performance;
- depression or a sense of isolation and in extreme cases, risk of suicide;
- physical injury; and/or
- reduced quality of home and family life (2017)."

It is really important to know how the complaint works in a company or government. It is necessary that all employees know the ethical code. One should know who to talk about when being harassed or bullied. How one should be protected. How to start a formal or informal complaint? How one should learn to behave with vexatious complaints. To have direct access with a supervisor, team leader or even above management. How the investigation may work or even how long it might take in order to be safe and secure. Who will lead the investigation? It is important to find how it is to be investigated. How the will decision take place?

Any kinds of Harassment is against Human Rights. There are various types of Harassment. The following are the types of harassment: Psychological Harassment at workplace, Sexual Harassment, other Racial Harassment, other religions Harassment, a certain group of people Undermining Discrimination, other unwanted touching. Other types can be offensive jokes, comments, pictures, or even cartoons. A few people may at first enjoy and laugh about these things but when it happens to them, they will realize the meaning.

When one goes though Psychological harassment, or any kind of Harassment, one should discuss their feeling with a close friend, then discuss with a superior, then file a complaint. Every claim should have an investigation. Then, depending the company or organization, one should try to have a mediation session. If mediation does not work find other solutions. In some areas, cities, Provinces, States or even countries, there are system that can go up to the commissionaire or even judges for Psychological Harassment or other types of harassment. Use all resources if they offer various kinds of services. In some places it is free, in others you may have to pay. If you want to deal with outside services instead of inside services, you may discuss this with a psychologist or other types of counselor. The professional can help you deal with any kind of situation that you may face at work.

# CHAPTER 4

# TOXIC RELATIONSHIPS

## Situations that can arise in a couple

The following paragraphs will discuss toxic relationships between boyfriends and girlfriends, husbands and wives, sons and daughters, and fathers and mothers. They will also cover people's reactions towards those they are in relationships with, and how these have affected and affect their pasts, presents, and futures. Certain situations leading to break-up or divorce and their possible causes are also discussed.

Different scenarios fall under different categories. Everyone lives their life based on experiences they've had or on examples they have seen. Those who have suffered in toxic relationships have been through psychological hardship and emotional pain. Every individual lives a different way and everyone has something to say. The following situations are based on real-life experiences.

The individuals who actually hurt their loved ones may or may not have realized how their actions hurt their partners. Many of them created toxic conditions that others could only live in up to a certain time. Metaphorically speaking, heat melts ice, meaning that people change with time and decide to stay away from those who will hurt them. Between couples where trust is not a keyword, love can become hate, and frustrations can turn to actions, sometimes leading to a need to solve the problem, or, alternately, to the creation of even greater tension. It takes time to heal, only time and proper guidance can help. In many Western countries, people are privileged to live in good conditions and to have enough support to find a way out of these relationships. Of course, when children are involved it makes everything more complicated. That being said, the Western societies allow for enough opportunity to develop oneself and to find a cure to our problem. There are enough resources and enough people who are willing to help others. It is simply a matter of choosing to do the right thing. It is important to remain wary of those who can bring harm into one's life. In other words, avoid toxic relationships.

## Situations

## Between friends

*The situation*

The two friends in question enjoy each other's company and have known each other well for a long time. One day both go to a party and meet a person of interest whom both wish to acquaint themselves with. One of the two friends gets more attention than the other. This creates disappointment in one and a sense of aggression towards the other. After getting to know the person of interest, the friend who got the most attention will try to change the conversation topic with the jealous friend in order to avoid tension between the two.

*The reaction*

It is obvious that the person who got all the attention will be very happy and the other will likely be upset. This may create a distance between the two friends and may incite a reaction in the short or long run. The person who did not get the attention commonly slowly withdraws and may lose respect for his or her friend based on what happened at the party.

*How it affects their pasts, presents and futures*

When two friends both desire the same person, many negative repercussions can arise. If the situation has occurred in the past, both may have different reactions and may feel uncomfortable talking about the individual in question. When discussing the issue with other friends, dissatisfaction could be voiced in either a loud or passive aggressive way to show resentment for what happened. If the situation is an ongoing concern, there is a chance that a conflict could arise and affect their friendship. In the long run, this could lead to talking in each other's back or to intolerance towards one another.

## Between husband and wife

*The situation*

The given couple argues over trivial and often irrelevant subjects and regularly have major disputes. Reasons could include not paying attention or a desire for control over the other. Mutual disrespect creates a negative environment.

*The reaction*

Disappointment and blame become a consequence of the situation. The man may blame the woman for not letting him touch her or for simply not showing him enough love. This may escalate and create a different atmosphere which could create unhappiness.

*How it affects their pasts, presents, and futures*

Not realizing their incompatibility in the past led to an unhappy union. Therefore, the present situation is one where both are looking for change. In this way, love became hate. The future will bring change and therefore the relationship will not be the same as it was in the past.

## Between boyfriend and girlfriend

*The situation*

Relationships have no age, no boundaries, no race, no religion, and no political aim. Almost every human on this Earth has encountered, at one time, a boy or girl who probably became their boyfriend or girlfriend. These relationships are most commonly formed in social contexts such as daycare, preschool, elementary school, high school, college, and university.

## The reaction

Some may have had many boyfriends or girlfriends, and may be attracted either to the same or opposite sex. Depending on the type of relationship, partners may communicate differently between each other based on sex and other factors. Therefore, having a boyfriend or girlfriend can incite different reactions among different people, some of which may be surprising. In western society, friends can be of both sexes but the difference between them is important.

## How it affects their pasts, presents, and futures

If, during childhood, there was a reason to differentiate between same sex or different sex, a person may find it difficult to alternate between both types of friends. A person may feel comfortable only with those of his/her sex or alternately, with those of the opposite sex.

# Between husbands, wives, boyfriends, and girlfriends

## The situation

The following is a commonality in the city of Montreal, in Quebec, Canada. Often, in when violent conflict within a couple occurs, one of the involved parties calls the police to solve the issue. This is natural to a certain extent. What is unfortunate, however, is that the caller had to involve the police in order to resolve their problem for them.

## The reaction

Many types of reactions are possible when one discovers that their partner sought support from the police, instead of solving the conflict maturely within the couple. The lack of trust within the couple is one issue, but even worse is the fact that one individual felt fear or a need for revenge. Involving the authorities could be a way to punish the other or for safety. If the latter is an issue, calling the police is always the way to go.

*How it affects their pasts, presents, and futures*

Once one has decided to call the police, the relationship is no longer the same. The love and affection that both involved parties had, whether it is between a woman and a man, a man and a man, or a woman and a woman, is deeply affected and may even be destroyed. The relationship, as it stands in the present moment, is changed forever. The future will lead either to breakup, temporary separation or divorce. The person who called the police will realize that this act damaged the life the couple was leading. That said, this change could also be for the better of each individual.

## Between husbands, wives, boyfriends, and girlfriends

*The situation*

Sometimes, in major disputes, couples physically fight each other. Conjugal violence and aggression can be mutual, or brought on either by the man or the woman to take advantage of the other. Antagonism increases to a point where it becomes almost a challenge to see who can hurt the other the most.

*The reaction*

A person may realize, after the fact, that what he/she did to the other was wrong and hurtful. The man may not realize that he hurt his partner and a woman may see that what she did against her man was not voluntary. This aggression will lead to increased tensions within the couple. After this kind of violence, frequency of verbal or physical attacks may increase.

*How it affects pasts, presents, and futures*

The relationship was affected from the moment the aggression occurred in the past. This has the consequence of breeding distrust and disrespect within the couple. This will lead the couple to decide whether they should keep the relationship alive or not. The decision in the present moment will lead to a better or worse future, depending on the choice taken. If conjugal violence is common within a couple, the relationship should be ended. Violence is not a solution, it is an aggressive action, and actions speak louder than words.

## Between husbands, wives, boyfriends, and girlfriends

*The situation*

When arguments occur frequently, limits should be put in place to reduce them. Arguments that arise as a consequence of not knowing when to end the relationship may put a pressure on a couple. Depending on the severity, some arguments that feature verbal abuse can be worse to bear than those featuring physical abuse. It is important to remember that conjugal abuse also includes verbal assault. It can happen that a victim is more hurt after verbal attack than physical attack.

*The reaction*

When being trapped by physical or verbal abuse, both members of the couple may face different issues. Their problems arise from the physical and verbal aspects of their conflicts, but also from the various combinations of actions and reactions that result from them. In western countries, physical and verbal abuse are seen as unacceptable by the society and the law, and there are both profit and non-profit organizations out there to solve these issues. With these in place, people are able to react quickly when violence occurs within a couple. It is a simple matter of filing a complaint and the necessary measures required to repair the problem are quickly put in place.

*How it affects pasts, presents, and futures*

If any kind of abusive action occurred in the past, the present and future states of the relationship will suffer. How much can an individual bear when his or her partner continually creates a negative atmosphere? Physical and verbal violence coupled with such an atmosphere adds stress to the affected person. Thus, a solution must be found. However, in the face of such conflict, judgment may be clouded, making it difficult to find the right way to solve the issue.

## Between husbands, wives, boyfriends, and girlfriends

*The situation*

Manipulation, insults, and verbal abuse in general is considered psychological abuse. In these situations, the one member of the couple takes advantage of the other to obtain what he/she wants. These contexts are often characterized by tense atmospheres, be it at home or in social situations.

*The reaction*

Men or women confronted with these issues quickly become upset and frustrated. An individual may tolerate this kind of treatment for a certain period of time, but the length varies between people and severity of the situation. Tolerance can be compared to blowing up a balloon without knowing exactly at which point the balloon will burst. The bursting of the balloon symbolizes the breaking point of the victim.

*How it affects pasts, presents, and futures*

In order to understand the reaction, the past needs to be evaluated. If there has been psychological harassment earlier in the relationship, the present and future reactions will be worse. Some people may be extremely upset due to what their partner blamed, abused, and punished them for. In the present, trust within the relationship will diminish. This will cause lack of faith in the other and a weakening of the bond between both partners. To help solve the problem, one member may seek help. This can be in the form of a family member, a friend, or a professional. This helps determine the future of the relationship.

## Between husbands, wives, boyfriends, and girlfriends

*The situation*

Arguments can arise when one partner constantly brings up a topic he/she is interested in. Though it is great to discuss matters that are of interest to one person, bringing up the subject over and again can seem like harassment. This is especially the case when the matter is a complaint directed at the other partner.

*The reaction*

Hearing one's partner complain over and again about the same issue is difficult to bear. This bring extra stress to both members, resulting in arguments. In these cases, discussing the topic one final time to prevent it from recurring is a good idea. If bringing it up often is hurtful, then one should refrain from doing so.

*How it affects pasts, presents, and futures*

Talking about the past too often can lead to arguments and a negative dynamic. Therefore, the present relationship will suffer from these constant reminders of the past. The future can be improved by remembering what triggered the problem and thus avoiding its recreation.

## Between sons, daughters, mothers, and fathers

*The situation*

When sons or daughters refuse to obey their parents' instructions, violence is used to resolve the problem, thus making the children suffer.

*The reaction*

Parents' aggressive behavior towards their children following disobedience can lead to a build-up of resentment in children. If a father, for example, is excessively strict and hits his son or daughter to earn respect, he may physically and emotionally damage his child. This instills fear and anxiety in children.

*How it affects pasts, presents, and futures*

Sons and daughters may learn abusive behaviors from their parents and later become more aggressive towards their siblings, friends, or future children.

## Between sons, daughters, mothers, and fathers

*The situation*

In cases of disobedience, parents punish their sons and daughters by verbally abusing them. Insults and unfair comparisons to other children or family members are used to degrade the child in question.

*The reaction*

Sons and daughters can start to hate their parents due to a sense of hurt brought on by verbal abuse.

*How it affects pasts, presents, and futures*

Children may begin to have low self-esteem, especially around adults and elders.

## Between husband and wife - divorce

*The situation*

Women often marry for money. Some women look to have relationships with successful men, even if only for a short period of time. When the relationship seems to be perfect, both parties become more serious and envision a future together. At this point, many men decide to propose to their significant others.

*The reaction*

The love and affection that is shown by the women in question convinces their husbands that they are in love. In these early stages, the relationship seems to be perfect. With time, however, unhappy wives begin bringing up issues and within a short time, either the husband or wife will file for divorce.

*How it affects pasts, presents, and futures*

Past memories and unhappy experiences will carry over into the present and future, leading to divorce. This can be very costly, especially in cases where the husband has much money, property, and assets. Children complicate situations further. Of course, all assets will be divided between the husband and wife, and the money-earner (often the man) will have to pay child support. This makes the future of all involved very difficult.

*Reason for divorce*

In this kind of situation, where the woman chose to marry and divorce as a means to earn money, it is clear that she loved money more than her partner.

## Between husband and wife - divorce

*The situation*

There could be various reasons why couples do not stay together. It could be due to a lack of common interests. These can include common love of movies, music or cooking. Discord can also be a result of secrecy between partners.

*The reaction*

In this situation there is something missing between both partners. Because of their few shared interests and lack of communication, arguments may arise within the couple.

*How it affects pasts, presents, and futures*

In order to truly understand each other, both individuals need to spend more time together and find interests they can share. The past cannot be changed but the present moment needs to be optimized to allow for a better future. If there is no communication within the couple, change will be difficult to achieve.

*Reason for divorce*

One of the main reasons for divorce is lack of communication. Partners do not communicate enough and fail to express their emotions towards their significant other.

## Between husband and wife - divorce

*The situation*

Relationships can be great, if they are done right. An issue that can arise within couples is that one forgets his or her role in that union. When a married person spends too much time with an unmarried friend, he/she may neglect certain aspects of his/her relationship.

*The reaction*

Neglecting one's relationship can be disastrous. If one partner does not give enough time to the other, many problems can arise.

*How it affects pasts, presents, and futures*

Marriage leads to a change in lifestyles. Husbands or wives may not appreciate that their significant other is spending more time with someone else. Many problems can arise from this. Current arguments and misunderstandings can cause even greater strife and distrust in the future.

*Reason for divorce*

Neglecting one's significant other to spend time with friends and failing to pay attention to the other's needs can lead to divorce.

## Between husband and wife

*The situation*

It is extremely important for both members of a couple to spend time together and to give each other enough attention. In order for the relationship between a man and a woman to stay strong, both parties need to pay attention to the other and to provide a listening ear and constructive feedback. Moreover, shared interests are also very important.

*The reaction*

If there is no attention given to either partner, then both will feel lost, neglected and empty. This could lead to the development of distance between both individuals. As a result, both will refrain from telling each other how they feel about the other.

*How it affects pasts, presents, and futures*

With lack of attention comes great distance, and eventually an aloofness towards the other's needs and emotions. Past actions will lead to empty bonds within the couple, which will affect the relationship in the future.

## Between husband and wife - divorce

*The situation*

Finance plays an important role in a couple's life together. It is important to be financially prepared to better face any money-related issues that could arise. Earning enough money can change a relationship. When only one member of the couple works and earns money, the other becomes a dependant. When both work, however, both can finance their life together and contribute to a higher income.

*The reaction*

With higher income comes greater financial responsibility. Once one is married, they have to provide not only for themselves, but for their family as well.

*How it affects pasts, presents, and futures*

Whereas one only had to provide for oneself in the past, marriage requires thinking about many others and planning in order to have financial security in the future.

*Reason for divorce*

Change in lifestyle can lead to change in marriage. If one partner is accustomed to being provided for, and suddenly is not, stress and hurt can arise. Unwillingness to share money one's significant other or family can have a negative impact on dependents. Money is a large factor in a relationship. Having more than once source of revenue is beneficial, and when one person does not contribute to the financial situation and takes advantage of the other, marriage is jeopardized.

## Between husband and wife - divorce

*The situation*

Immigration is a word that brings hope and dreams to many people. It suggests a new beginning in a new land. Sometimes individuals who have left their home country return long enough to find a bride or groom. In this situation, many people will do anything to be selected as the best candidate.

*The reaction*

When the landed immigrant brings with them a wife or husband from their homeland into their current country of residence, the future seems bright and exciting. The chosen partner appears to be incredibly fortunate and may notice how living in a new country has changed their new husband or wife.

*How it affects pasts, presents, and futures*

Before immigrating, many people have unrealistic expectations and beliefs about the country they are moving to. Past impressions form reactions to current situations, but as immigrants begin to understand their new surroundings, these ideas may change and the future of that person can be extremely difficult and different than expected.

## *Reason for divorce*

Someone who has lived differently may feel unsettled when being in a new country. The changes may be too great for the person in question. Expectations brought on by the husband or wife before marriage could be entirely different than reality. This disappointment can lead to divorce.

## Between husband and wife - divorce

### *The situation*

Sex is important for the maintenance of healthy relationships. Showing one's partner that he or she is special during intimate moments can make or break a relationship. What happens when one's partner is not satisfied sexually? In this case, relationships may not work or may require some work and attention.

### *The reaction*

Sexual dissatisfaction can break a relationship or provoke a partner to cheat. Lack of pleasure, or inability to reach orgasm during sexual activities may lead to discord within the couple.

### *How it affects pasts, presents, and futures*

Past experiences involving lack of pleasure can be very disappointing. These can affect the current state of the relationship due to loss of desire and lack of confidence. This, in turn, can destroy the future of the relationship because one might have chosen to cheat on the other, or may have chosen to leave the other.

*Reason for divorce*

Lack of sexual pleasure can lead to tension, cheating and breaking up. When pleasure is absent, one or both parties may feel discouraged and may lose motivation. Of course, reactions changed depending on the relationship in question, and not all couples feel the need for divorce.

## Between husbands, wives, boyfriends, and girlfriends - break-up and divorce

*The situation*

A boy starts dating a girl. Both are teenagers and are exploring what love is. They enjoy each other's company and share many friends. Eventually, however, the boy meets another girl who is of interest to him.

*The reaction*

The boy's girlfriend does not appreciate the presence of that girl. She feels jealous. The girlfriend begins to antagonize the other girl. Soon, her boyfriend and the new girl exchange phone numbers and begin text messaging each other. Many months later, he decides to date the new girl at the same time as his current girlfriend.

*How it affects pasts, presents, and futures*

A man who decides to cheat on a woman as a teenager will likely also cheat during his marriage. What one should ask his- or herself is if it is worth it to cheat on their partner for a passing fling. Marriage is designed to be for life, and flings are not. There is no reason why a stranger should come between life partners.

*Reason for break-up or divorce*

Cheating leads to break-up or divorce.

## Between husbands, wives, boyfriends, and girlfriends - break-up and divorce

*The situation*

Parenting and marriage do not necessarily go hand in hand. A man or woman may choose to begin a relationship with someone who already has children. They seek to accept and to be accepted by the family they are looking to be a part of.

*The reaction*

It is rarely easy to begin a relationship with someone who has children. Sometimes, the new partner is not fit to be with the children in question, or may simply not get along with them.

*How it affects pasts, presents, and futures*

It is better not to get involved in a relationship with another person's children because they may not always respect you as a person who has authority over them. Sometimes if one gets involved, they begin to feel attached to the child that is not theirs. This can affect a person emotionally later on. That being said, there are many cases of successful step-parenting to inspire oneself from.

## Between husbands, wives, boyfriends, and girlfriends

*The situation*

Physical and/or mental abuse is one of the major factors which can lead to failed relationships.

*The reaction*

The situation within the couple can create conflict and lead to tension and stress. Every facet of a person is tested in these kinds of relationships.

*How it affects pasts, presents, and futures*

Often, the victimized partner is forced to remain silent through the use of intimidation and manipulation. This kind of unhealthy relationship has little chance of continuing on for long. The present self is nothing like the past self of the abusing partner. The victim may wonder why they ever got into this relationship to begin with, but could not have known this side of their partner. These observations consequently change the future of the relationship forever.

## Between husbands, wives, boyfriends, and girlfriends

*The situation*

Attraction is an important part of being in a relationship. When a partner does not give enough time and attention to his/her significant other, a gap in communication between the two grows and causes one to lose interest in the other.

*The reaction*

Physical and verbal communication gaps cause both parties to express themselves to one another less and less.

*How it affects pasts, presents, and futures*

It is only in retrospect that one will realize that they reacted in a different way with their significant other and that this caused distance. Their behaviour will affect the couple in the future and dealing with various situations will be increasingly difficult, especially if any children are involved.

## Between husbands, wives, boyfriends, and girlfriends

*The situation*

Infidelity is a commonly discussed issue with regards to problem relationships. It is normal that a man or a woman is attracted to other people. However, uncontrolled attraction when in a relationship can severely harm or even ruin one's bond with their partner.

*The reaction*

When a relationship is ruined, each individual reacts differently. When one discovers the true self of his or her partner, they will first feel very hurt, and then wonder why they began a relationship with this person in the first place.

*How it affects pasts, presents, and futures*

They're relationship between boyfriend, girlfriend ends up and breakup or even between husband and wife turns up in divorce. One did not realized that when starting cheating their partner the relationship might end and in present and in the future they may have a bad reputation between their community and may be seen as cheaters and dishonest.

## Between husbands, wives, boyfriends, and girlfriends

*The situation*

Some negative situations involve one partner humiliating the other. He or she lacks empathy towards the other and constantly describes how inadequate the victim of these attacks is. These insults are often said in front of other people.

*The reaction*

The target in these situations often suffers and feels inferior to his/her partner, who is always boasting his/her own qualities and putting the victim down. It always seems to the target that their partner is making him- or herself out to be the king or queen of everything.

*How it affects pasts, presents, and futures*

The victims may undergo humiliation for a long time, especially when they have children with the abuser. In the past of their relationships, things may have been different, so the victims may not have known this would happen. Once the humiliated individuals realize the true colors of their partners, they have to evaluate the current state of affairs and make changes for their futures. Regret and uncertainty unfortunately always remain a part of the future for these people.

## Between husbands, wives, boyfriends, and girlfriends - break-up and divorce

*The situation*

It is difficult to live with someone who is constantly harassing his or her partner. This is, again, an attitude whose purpose is to keep the other under his/her control. The victimized individual is subjected to his/her partner's constant fault-finding, complaints, criticisms and frequent sarcastic remarks.

*The reaction*

Typical reactions include a loss of feeling and respect for the antagonist. Tendencies to harass are possibly more common in women than men. For both sexes harassment can be difficult to handle.

*How it affects pasts, presents, and futures*

The suffering individual can only tolerate harassment up to a certain extent. Showing mercy and understanding becomes increasingly difficult for this person and sooner or later breakup becomes the most viable option. Patience eventually runs out, as does the future of the relationship.

## Between husbands, wives, boyfriends, and girlfriends

*The situation*

Jealousy in a relationship is common. Some suggest that in some cases, this phenomenon is caused by mental illness. Jealousy can cause damage in a relationship between boyfriends, girlfriends, husbands and wives. It can also destroy marriages. Jealousy can arise in a couple when one discovers that the reason they are not receiving enough attention is because their partner is seeing someone else.

*The reaction*

A man or a woman may flirt with another with the sole purpose of creating jealousy in the relationship to manipulate his/her partner. This can be in the aim of getting more attention. This type of manipulation can cause relationships to be broken.

*How it affects pasts, presents, and futures*

It is wrong to purposely create jealousy because this can lead to resentment in the short and long runs. This can even push the manipulated partner to exact revenge on the manipulator, which is bad for any relationship.

## Between husbands, wives, boyfriends, and girlfriends

*The situation*

Pathological lying is very tricky to deal with when it is present in a relationship. When a partner constantly lies to the other, it imperils the entire union.

*The reaction*

Jeopardizing a relationship by lying leads nowhere. Often, telling the truth is necessary and allows for trust within a couple. It is important to avoid telling lies as much as possible. Lying can break friendships and romantic liaisons.

*How it affects pasts, presents, and futures*

Lying to one's partner leads to distrust. It is so hard to build trust and it can be lost to lying very fast. If a partner has lied to their significant other in the past, the relationship suffers in the present and trust is lost.

However, it can also be detrimental to tell the truth all the time as it can emotionally hurt one's partner.

## Between husbands, wives, boyfriends, and girlfriends

*The situation*

Arguments and quarrels are natural within couples. However, it is necessary to be able to control one's action and behaviours, even in these moments. Broken relationships arise when frequency and severity of the quarrels are too great to bear. When both individuals want things to go a certain way and they do not, one or both partners may begin an argument to take control of the situation.

*The reaction*

When each one wants to have their way, neither can agree on a compromise. This is hard on any relationship. Arguments may start with shouting, leading to loss of self-control and, sometimes, physical violence. This often creates even more tension and leads to emotional damage.

*How it affects pasts, presents, and futures*

Being a part of a relationship is never easy. It is very challenging. Past arguments can create more arguments in the future. When one partner seeks to exact revenge on the other because of past issues, the current state of the relationship takes a hit. It is usually better to compromise and to find a solution in order to feel better in the future.

## Between husbands, wives, boyfriends, and girlfriends

*The situation*

Some partners unfortunately often compare their significant others with someone else they think is 'better' at certain things. These people will continuously weigh their partners against others.

*The reaction*

Reactions typically involve frustration and conflict between both individuals. The accused partner may develop an inferiority complex. The accuser may persist and try to emphasize how other people are adhere to better standards than his/her partner.

*How it affects pasts, presents, and futures*

No one likes to be compared. One should not be compared to another because all individuals live and think differently. Harmony and acceptance should be at the center of any relationship. Constant comparison of one's partner could lead to future resentment and destructive criticism in return. Receiving a similar kind of treatment in the future would make the accuser realize how painful comparing one to another really is.

## Between husbands, wives, boyfriends, and girlfriends

*The situation*

Being involved with a significant other means introducing him or her to one's family. It may happen that either one or many family members do not like one's boyfriend or girlfriend. Each family member and every friend has a say. Either they like him or her or they do not. It is in the latter case that a relationship can take a hit.

*The reaction*

Listening to one's family's or friends' points of view may affect how one sees their partner. This can sometimes be negative, leading to break-up. What to do in these situations comes down to personal choice. Arguments that arise from doubts planted in one's mind by others can affect any relationship.

*How it affects pasts, presents, and futures*

When one's family or friends do not get along with one's partner, it may seem that the only thing to do is to end the relationship. Otherwise, a negative environment can make both partners feel uncomfortable and insecure. Once the choice to let go of one's partner because of duty towards one's family is made, the future is simple.

## Between husbands, wives, boyfriends, and girlfriends

*The situation*

In some situations, individuals choose to move away from their partners because of work, family, immigration, or for personal advancement.

*The reaction*

A proverb says "out of sight, out of mind". Is that really the case? Some relationships actually show that partners can be surprisingly devoted to one another. However, in some cases, one partner may try to wait for the other, but after a certain period of time, decides to find someone else to fill the place of the other in the meantime.

*How it affects pasts, presents, and futures*

The future can be simple: some choose to continue seeing another until their partner returns. Some decide to wait until their partners invite them to come live with them in another city. Some couples wait and others break. There are obviously couples who seem to work out their relationships even if there is a distance between them.

## Between husbands, wives, boyfriends, and girlfriends

*The situation*

Some people will always prioritize work over their partners. Their career seems to be more important than their relationship. Some spend a lot of time at work and forget that they have a partner who is waiting at home them. That being said, it is important to have a stable job but it is also important to spend time with one's family and loved ones.

*The reaction*

When these situations arise, arguments may occur within the couple and even within the family. Families and significant others may feel that the person in question is not giving them enough time. This can create a distance between boyfriends, girlfriends, husbands, and wives.

*How it affects pasts, presents, and futures*

The fact that there was a distance caused by one-sided neglect leads to a change in the current relationship. There might be no bad intention from the person who is working too much but he/she may lose patience and fail to see how supporting his/her family financially is neglectful.

## Between husbands, wives, boyfriends, and girlfriends

*The situation*

When relationships begin there are many good times and a few bad times. With time, arguments become more frequent. This becomes a bother and finding a solution to this problem is difficult; one may not know what to do.

*The reaction*

Verbal fights break out for multiple reasons. This may bother partners enormously and being the realization that these go nowhere. Confusion and hurt arise and it is often difficult to understand why one's other half is so aggressive. However, lack of patience leads to continued arguments.

*How it affects pasts, presents, and futures*

Constant argument becomes similar to harassment and leads to a desire to separate oneself from one's partner. The verbal fighting creates tension which have a negative impact on moods and psyche. A solution is key to resolving chronic quarrelling.

# Causes for break-up

In any kind of relationship, one might wonder what the causes for break-up are. The following describes possible motivations for ending a relationship.

First of all, physical and mental abuse are obvious reasons for wanting to end any union. Partners who punish and cause their significant others anguish are not worth keeping. People want to feel loved and secure. People do not like to be manipulated.

Secondly, looks are a big factor in continuing relationships. If one gains significant weight or for some reason loses their looks, their partner might lose attraction for them and, consequently, leave them.

Thirdly, cheating or infidelity are sure ways to end a relationship. No one likes to be cheated. People search for trust within their couple and most believe in monogamy. Humans seek to bond with those who make them feel secure.

Fourthly, no one likes to be humiliated in front of others. If one hears that their partner is badmouthing them to others, they may feel these are grounds enough for separation. For example, saying to others that your partner is "good for nothing" won't solve anything, but it will certainly harm your relationship.

Fifthly, constant complaints or criticisms are hurtful and may deeply affect an individual. Healthy couples do not nag their partners.

Sixthly, jealousy can break bonds between partners. Jealousy is something to avoid when seeking a serious and loving relationship.

Next, lying to one's partner is also destructive. Once one begins lying to their partner, it could become a bad habit. Strong and solid relationships rely on honesty. Lying to surprise one's partner is one thing, but lying to see someone else is destructive.

Furthermore, arguments and quarrels are not constructive methods for communication. Fighting can hurt children or others in a couple's immediate environment. In some cases, a couple's reputation in a neighborhood could even be tarnished due to overly loud arguing. Sometimes, depending the country, province, state, or city, the police could also get involved.

Moreover, motives behind getting into a relationship are important to consider., For example, it is crucial to know whether one's partner is with the other for love, or simply for status or money.

Lastly, comparisons between partners never brings any good. If one's partner only puts him/her down, then it could mean that that individual would prefer to be with someone else. Comparisons to others demonstrate someone's desire to live a different life. This will therefore be a burden on the union. As a result the relationship will often end.

## Marriage and conjugal relationships

It is a happy sight to see two people together. With a marriage, a couple chooses to show the world their commitment to each other. It is a promise to be faithful, show care, love, affection, and compassion for each other. They will share the same house and the same bed, have a faithful sexual relationship and be true to each other, all while keeping the right attitude and remaining honest to one another by sharing their thoughts, values, and morals. Couples have to be open to each other in their personal conversations. Preparing meals and doing domestic work together is part of marriage, as is surprising each other once in a while. It is also important for couples to take care of each other during times of illness. A relationship will come out strong when it is put to the test.

Keeping on top of domestic chores is part of married life but so are invitations to participate in various activities held by the community or by friends. This can enhance and diversify the relationship to include so much more than just one's spouse. Maintaining a good understanding among family members is essential in maintaining a happy relationship. Moreover, understanding one's partner's financial situation can take pressure off the relationship, as it helps people work together. One has to value his or her partner's opinion when spending money on valuable gifts and necessary household items. Both partners need to have a financial agreement and must be able to compromise to better balance their budgets. Ownership assets needs to be pre-determined to avoid any kinds of upset. In this way, should the need for separation or divorce arise, ownership is already made clear and will not cause issues. Children are another matter entirely and both parents have equal responsibility towards them. The roles could just as easily be reversed, however.

What causes a relationship to fell apart? Usually it is small misunderstandings that go unresolved and that lead to bigger, more destructive fights. If there is a serious problem, both parties need work together to fix the relationship; otherwise it will fail. If they do not, both partners may become tired of their relationship and lose trust for one another. However, many couples do not want to break up if there is a child or many children involved. In these cases, they need to understand each other and share their thoughts, feelings and worries in order to better function as a couple. It is natural to make silly mistakes and, in these instances, one should ask the other for forgiveness. Cruel words can hurt one's feelings or even break another's heart. Knowing each other's limits is the most important thing when trying to fix a relationship.

What happened in the past of a relationship should be kept in the past. A couple should move forward by acknowledging what happened and being truthful to each other. Keeping an open mind and working as a team will open many doors. This will give the couple a second chance to value and respect each other. In order to move on, both parties need to agree on what they want. Do both want to maintain the relationship? Are they willing to change their bad habits to do so? Do they want to fix their misunderstandings? It takes both people in a relationship to fix or to destroy it. Both need to ask themselves what exactly the source of conflict is in order to prevent it happening again. When dealing with one's doubts, worries, confusions, and criticisms towards the other, one has to think about the future and plan accordingly. If both parties want to be together, both need to work and find a structure that will help them maintain a healthy relationship. By planning for the future, the couple will make progress.

## Control and addiction

Other potential reasons why couples choose to file for divorce include repeated losses of control and addictions to drugs, alcohol, or gambling. Loss of control refers to abusive behavior towards one's spouse, family, or friends. It can also include uncontrolled spending. Addictions that cause one to neglect their family can lead to divorce. In some cultures, individuals are required to send money to their families. To do this, some may take money from their partners. If this occurs too often, or if one individual is dishonest about their financial situation by storing their money in a secret bank account, the other partner may choose to file for divorce.

## Trust and Love

It is normal to have varying feelings toward someone. Sometimes, over time, people change and partners may fall in and out of love with each other. It can happen that one simply no longer has feelings for their partner, because of lack of affection or attraction. Trust could also slowly be lost over time. If one's partner lied too many times, then trust within the relationship dies out. People may make stupid mistakes but with time it can be reparable, if both parties are mature enough to rebuild trust and seek mutual understanding.

## Employment problems and family obligations

When there are family obligations it can be very difficult to combine personal and family life. The spouse may wish for extra attention or time as a couple. On the other hand, his or her family may wish to see more of him/her. Time invested with one's family can take the form of grocery shopping or simply running errands for them. Unfortunately, it can happen at times that one's partner forces them to choose between spending time with him/her or one's family. This kind of ultimatum can force one to make a bad decision. Therefore, it is important to remember that understanding is beneficial to each partner when it comes to balancing family and marital obligations. Taking the time to make everybody happy can be demanding, but is a good thing to do. In order to successfully achieve this, it is important to take the time to prioritize one's values. For example, if finances are a struggle, then these need to be prioritized, because if they go unattended, they could affect a couple's relationship.

## Lack of communication and personality problems

It is important to have a good communication within the couple. Often, when partners argue, both sides only half listen to what the other is saying. In order to better communicate, both parties need to listen to and acknowledge each other. Problems and misunderstandings occur when there is lack of communication. Misunderstandings are caused when one or both partners fail to show respect, appreciation or loyalty to the other. It is necessary between both individuals to value each other in order to achieve successful communication. Marriages can fail when there is a lack of communication.

There may also be a link between poor communication and personality problems. One partner may have certain negative personality traits and this can cause marital strife. Some examples of negative personality traits include laziness, rudeness, pickiness, arrogance, self-centredness, bossiness, and thoughtlessness. Having negative traits such as these, if unsolved, can severely damage or break a relationship. On the other hand, some positive personality traits include honesty at all costs, a sense of responsibility, perfectionism, adaptability, compatibility to others, ambition, compassion, and understanding. Another crucial personality trait when repairing a relationship is patience. It is a virtue after all.

## Infidelity and incompatibility

At first it might seem fun or thrilling to cheat on one's spouse. It might be exhilarating to have a secret lover with whom one enjoys having sexual intercourse. This person may become very special to the unfaithful partner, and though the goal was not to have emotional attachment to this person, doing so might add emotional pleasure to the physical pleasure. Being with someone else while having a husband or wife can create distance within a marriage. Cheating and dishonesty towards one's spouse is unfaithfulness. Years of work on a marriage can be destroyed by a few minutes of forbidden pleasure. It is very difficult to build a castle with cards but it is very easy to destroy it. Faithfulness makes for strong relationships.

Unhappiness can be due to incompatibility. There could be many reasons why couples do not fully 'click'. It is not always obvious to realize that partners are incompatible. It can take years. The same reasons that brought two people together do not always apply over time. People, emotions, and tastes all change with time. Therefore, things one may have appreciated in the past could suddenly stop doing so with time. The same concept applies to individuals' feelings towards their significant others. This is why some may feel, over time, that they are no longer compatible with their partners. Separation suddenly becomes a viable option, as is accepting one's spouse for who they are and cherishing the relationship built with them, and choosing to 'go with the flow' of life.

# CHAPTER 5

# MARRIAGE AND THERAPY

## Marriage and Therapy

What is marriage? Marriage is a relationship between two individuals, commonly referred to as husband and wife. However, modern laws have come to recognize the legal marriage between same-sex couples, more commonly referred to as gay or lesbian couples. However, for the purposes of this writing, the author has chosen to focus on traditional heterosexual relationships.

Upon being married, the relationship of a couple becomes official, permanent, and publicly notarized. Unofficial requirements for marriage may include compassion, passion, affection, mutual trust, respect, honesty, and caring. In many cases, married couples may have children, and eventually take on the role of grandparent. However, in recent centuries, divorce has become an increasingly common occurrence among married couples. The reasons for divorce vary; some couples may no longer find themselves attracted to each other, while others may have been unfaithful and as such broken the bonds of matrimony. Still others may find it difficult to share the same values and faith, or prefer to live alone. However, before seeking divorce it is often recommended to seek marriage counseling, to see if the issues within the relationship have the potential to be resolved.

The following information will focus on how to help and understand the process of couples, or marriage, counseling. It will provide you with an overview of various topics that you may face in real time and real life. Certain situations may change or may no longer exist depending on the time that you are reading this.

# Financial conflicts

Among the many conflicts between husband and wife, money dependency is a big issue. In the modern century, mostly the twenty first century, humans are brainwashed with money. People are becoming crazy for money - anything you want to do requires money, even marriage counselling.

In most third world countries, men work and women stay home. Men bring money and women take care of family. When only one partner works, one may not see the value of money the way one should see it. Life is becoming more and more expensive; one need to work to buy foods, clothes, accessories, cellular bills, home phone, cable bills, electricity, water, furniture, car expense, travel cost, gas, pay their house either renting it or having their own house by paying mortgage, some have personal loans or business loans - the list seems to never end. Some can effort it while others may not. When only men make money the female partner may not see where the money is going. It is also become hard for one person to take care of the full family expenses.

Obviously when both couples work the finances are balanced in most of the time. However, when the finances are not balanced, conflict may occur. Some women may think that their husband is being too cheap by controlling the finances; when a woman desire something and the man is not capable of providing her with her desires, this might create drama and conflict between them. Women also have needs and they also need some sort of revenue to live. Some men make money and desire to give to the women and they deal with the expense. Other men want to control their finance. Overtime, you will notice that in most of the cast if you do not provide enough money to your partner the relationship may become very narrow. Sometime, you may see that either your partner or your children has stolen money from you. When you choose to socialized with other people you will need to be prepared to be open minded. You will need to share money with your family by buying them stuffs. Your partner may see other friends or strangers happy and well dressed to impress or in a very luxury way. Hence you do not dress her well, in this situation it might create conflict.

Sometimes, it is beneficial to avoid having too many friends, as this may cause unnecessary expenditures on your part – through social gatherings and such – while in other cases having friends may be a therapeutic benefit to your life. In some instances, it is the situation of your surroundings that is the toxic element in your life. Your friends or family members may attempt to push their beliefs upon you, which may conflict with your values or way of life.

On the other hand, when both man and woman work, life can be beautiful and harmonious. In this case, both can take care of their finances. Children will be healthier and happier as a result, as parents are more open to buying their children gifts. Women can understand the value of money so do the men. They share a budget with dreams of buying toys such as car, motorcycle, boat or other types of transportation or even condos or houses between husband and wife. Both can buy things for each other or even for their loved one. When both work, both understand the family budget. Things may change overtime, when one spends too much money within a short period of time. One may become drug addicted, or alcoholic, or spending in gambling. This is toxic and will create excessive stress for the family members and couples, which might lead for future conflict some even separation or divorced.

## No sex

When there is less sexual attraction or even less sexual intercourse between a couple, the relationship seems to fall apart. We do not feel the same as we did at the beginning of the relationship and couples may seem to find fault in each other more readily. The fact is that strong sexual affection builds strong relationships. When you feel complete after the intercourse you will feel happiness in you. When you will feel agitated, rush to come, there is no fun or simply you just can't enjoy sexually, it might get frustrating. Your partner may also feel ashamed or say that you cannot perform well enough to please her or him.

The *Huffington Post* published a piece on recent research undertaken on men, and how often they make love with their partners. "Perhaps the best data about how frequently couples have sex comes from the Kinsey Institute. A survey of more than 2,300 married men found that nearly 46 percent of 18- and 24-year-olds, and 37 percent of 25- to 29-year-olds, said they had sex two to three times per week, compared to just 27 percent of 30- to 39-year-olds, 20 percent of 40- to 49-year-olds and 15 percent of 50- to 59-year-olds. In a similar vein, 18- to 24-year-olds were far more likely than their older counterparts to have sex four or more times per week, while 18- to 29-year-olds were the age group least likely to have sex only monthly, or a few times per year" (2017).

When you are having sex because you think you need to, it may begin to feel like a routine. In many cases, when a man is suffering from depression, he will not feel willing to have sex. It will take a longer amount of time and stimulation for him to achieve an erection, often causing frustration in one or both parties. In some instances, a man can think about other things while having sex with his partner, which may allow him to relax and become calmer during intercourse.

Another issue during sexual intercourse for men can be erectile dysfunction and premature ejaculation. These occurrences often result in frustration; men may withdraw from their partner due to fear that their partner will become disappointed in them or lose interest. One cause for this may be due to age; when a man enters his forties, the testosterone levels decrease over time, resulting in a low sex drive.

Stress may also cause sexual dysfunction. The stress of making a large amount of money or having an otherwise successful career can affect a man's personal life. Changes in mood may result from work burdens, which in turn affect the relationship. It is important that couples make each other feel important, no matter what may be happening at work or during the work day. However, this may not always be the case; men may simply be suffering from fatigue, and not have the energy to participate in intercourse. When a man does not feel his best, he will be less willing to participate in sexual intercourse. However, if this occurs for more than a few weeks, it is important to consult a therapist or physician. It is important to take your time during intercourse, to create a strong bond and build a strong relationship.

## Cheating

Cheating is a sign of unhealthy relationship. But why would someone cheat? Both men and women cheat within relationships. Aside from character and personality issues, there are a multitude of individual reasons as to why someone would cheat.

Not feeling satisfaction within a relationship – whether it be emotional, mental, or physical satisfaction – may cause tension and stress which may result in a partner attempting to find this satisfaction elsewhere. Some individuals who cheat also report feeling bored, as they do not find enough love or adventure within their relationship. Some women may require their partner to be more romantic, or good with words. Many individuals may become frustrated in their marital relationships, lacking empathy and not caring about the consequences of their infidelity.

There are also situational reasons for cheating; an individual can put their partner in a different situation which might be for good reason or even bad one, just to see the reaction of the partner. This level of manipulation is harmful to a healthy relationship. It is important to acknowledged and address all unresolved issues between couples in a relationship. A lack of communication may result in difficulties in understanding the needs and desires of one's partner. We often do things just to please our partner. When one does not value one's partner, they may begin to feel unappreciated. This will have a negative impact on the relationship, and result in tension.

Nobody is perfect, and oftentimes we tend to be little arrogant in front of our partner especially when we see that there is a chance to show off and to feel superior in front of our partner. Some people wait for a good opportunity to take action; he or she may want to cheat but do not until they find reasons to start cheating. It's awkward - when things seem to go wrong, everything go wrong. Having excessive conflict between a couple can also be another reason why marriages fail. Pointing out every single thing that a person does wrong, or that you do not like, is not healthy and is oftentimes extremely toxic behaviour. Both men and women make mistakes, therefore it is not necessary to tell the other person what he or she is doing and discouraging them just because you do not like that way it is done.

Never encourage one to cheat or challenge one to cheat; he or she will have doubt and may look for excitement and passion somewhere else. Friends or strangers may also get a self-esteem boost from others. This will lead to them finding themselves superior to you and having the desire to try for change. They will look somewhere else until they find what they are looking for.

Some people may be unsure as to when to end a relationship, result in the creation of an unhealthy environment for his or her partner. Cheating in this case may become an exit strategy within a marriage. Human beings are not perfect; oftentimes one can find themselves capable of providing more attention to a new partner while neglecting their spouse or significant other. One will purposely neglect and make their partner feel uncomfortable so that he or she can feel superior; making the rules or regulations in the relationship.

In some cases, when a new baby is born, a partner may feel jealous because they do not have enough attention or affection from their partner. Jealousy leads to various types of uncanny behaviors which can create tension between couples. When escalated, this may lead to separation. In some instances, before marriage an individual may act differently in a relationship than they do when they finally get married. Some people may rush to get married but then find themselves feeling trapped because they later feel that they did not make the right decision. Once they realize this – after marriage – they may find out that it is too late to take a step back and analyze their relationship.

Insecurity is also another reason why one may cheat. A partner may give hints to the other that something or other is wrong in the relationship, or that they are not pleased with an aspect of their partnership. If this is not solved, oftentimes one will succumb to cheating. If this is the case, and a partner discovers the acts of infidelity, the desire for revenge may occur. In many instances, upon discovering their partner's infidelity many individuals will resort to cheating in turn, as a way of "getting back" at them. If you cannot trust your partner, you may resort to such acts in order to make them suffer.

In some cases, people cheat on their partner in order to get out of a bad financial situation. If you have financial stress, you may resort to anything to get us of trouble. Therefore, oftentimes the cheating partner may be someone with greater funds than one's spouse or partner. Not being able to pay rent, mortgage, or car load – or simply living with a high cost of life – may lead some individuals to find other means of income through sexual relationships.

It is important to think twice before committing to any adulterous relationships, as this will – almost always – negatively affect one's long-term partnership. You may have a long term relationship with someone for ten years, then suddenly decide to sleep with someone else, destroying the ten years of commitment that you gave. In some cases, sex addiction can lead to infidelity, due to one's insatiable sexual appetites. It is necessary to practice self control.

Knowing your personal limits is highly important in a relationship. When aging, women may face hormonal changes and this could affect the relationship. Not willing to make love or too much willing to make love can be a problem. When seeing changes with a girl, then a woman, then a wife, and then a grandmother, just these four words will lead you for hormonal changes. Same thing for men -a boy, then a man, then a husband and then a grandfather. Furthermore, when having long-term relationship with someone in the same time being married to someone else can become dramatic. Who should you let go once caught. Your wife or your secret lover? It is very important to be honest with your partner; just one mistake can ruin your life, especially if you have children. If you decide to give your partner a chance, you must make sure to set boundaries and not to allow them to become too self-centered. It is good to think about yourself sometimes, but it is important to keep in mind that in a partnership you are responsible not only for yourself, but for the well-being of your partner and your children.

In short; do not put yourself in a situation where you will hurt your partner, your children and, in the end, yourself. Regardless of what you do with your life, it is always best to be honest with your partner. If both of you are honest, then you will share a happier and healthier life with your mate and your children.

## Poor communication

Poor communication will always be a problem in our society; it damages a relationship; it can break couple apart. As the Chinese proverb states: "Trouble comes from the mouth". If one cannot express their thoughts properly, he or she will have hard time in explaining something that has to be done or one preventing themselves from doing something that cause harm. In this case, how can you understand your partner if your partner does not understand you? If you are hurt, you need to express yourself. If you cannot express yourself, your partner will have a hard time following you. Some may say "love" is universal and has many languages. However, you need to understand your partners' language in order to participate in an argument. Who is right when you cannot even tell if *you* are wrong or right? You should not focus only on body language, but also take the time to listen to your partner and share the same feelings and words between the both of you. Saying something from our mouth and expressing something from our bodies has different meaning. If you truly love someone, try to learn their language as well. You may feel more love when you understand their value and expression. For example, if you take the word "Love" and see all the synonyms you will find the following words: "Dealing, Dear, Dearest, Sweetheart, Honey, Affection, Adoration, Friendship, Tenderness, and Feeling". When expressing love which words are most meaningful for you when your lover mention one of the words above? It should make you feel special. These words make people feel good when used to express their point of view. Remember, do not give directives if you or your partner cannot understand them. When telling someone something, he or she may feel reluctant to be ordered around. Some examples are the phrases, "you should...", "you better...", "you must...", "you ought to...", "you have to..." These statements can cause harm and make one angry especially, if there is a communication gap. It is also important to not generalize a person's behavior or character in a negative way. Example: "never", "everyone", "again", "every time", or other types of words that might make you feel uncomfortable should be avoided in these conversations. Furthermore, you should not pressure an individual; never force someone to do something because you might have no choice as well later in life to do something that will be asked of you in turn. One should always recognize one's emotion, either positive or negative, and appreciate soft comments and allow nice feedback. Let your partner feel you - let your partner say what he or she feels for you.

## Anger

Anger causes destruction in a relationship. In a relationship, couples are very close to each other, and often each person has different expectation from their close one. Everyone has a limit for something, and one should be careful not to push that limit. People do not like to be forced to do something. There are various types of anger that vary depending on the character and personality of the individual. Some reasons why people can be angry toward their loved one are: due to interests, behaviors, jealousy, dominance, power, being confused within themselves, and becoming critical and short-tempered with your partners. Often when one is angry it will hurt your feelings, change your mood, and make you more negatively excited. Some people keep anger within themselves, and later may feel negative due to bottling up their emotions within themselves. It is really important to let things go; the longer you keep negative emotions inside of you, the greater the change there is to think about the situation and why you are so angry. When you express your frustration in your partner, you may be able to deal with the situation for a certain time, but he or she will bring that thing later to you, either by making you angrier or by using you in a different way. You may not realize at the beginning, but the truth is that angry people can create more enemies. Even though you share the same house, same room, same bed, your partner will be the first one to be your enemy. One may often say things out of rage and this can transform in a violent way, which will lead to negative action. When both you and your partner are in rage, both of you are out of control - this will have an impact in your behaviors. Later, one might feel anxiety or fear that one gets violent. If you lose control you lost your mind and it is very hard to control one's temper. Depending on how angry you might become, your actions may give a wrong and bad impression of you. People may judge you by your behaviors but not by how or what you truly are. This will lead you toward a bad reputation within your friend circle or even among your family members. The person that you loved so much suddenly will be against you and may even call the police. Moreover, it will break your heart. In short, anger has the potential to cause aggression and even violence.

## Lack of love

When you begin to notice a lack of love in your relationships you should start to question its elements. All relationships require good maintenance and attention; it is important to pay attention to your loved ones. Without a solid intimate bond between you and your partner, your strength as a couple may fade if you do not care for the non-physical elements of your relationship. It is important that you care for your partner as an individual, and not only focus on the desire of the sexual aspects of your relationship; you must maintain meaningful communication. Without this level of intimacy, your marriage or relationship may feel as if you are spending time and sharing a bed with a stranger and not your partner. There are several common reasons why you may find yourself feeling less attracted to your partner – or why your partner may find themselves feeling less attracted to you. Usually, women may find themselves feeling less attractive, and worry that this will affect how their husband perceives them as they age. They no longer view themselves as being as attractive as they were when they were young. Furthermore, some men may treat their partners as personal property, despite any changes in how they perceive their partner. Even if they previously did not view their partner in this way, time may alter their perceptions; they may flirt with other women because they are no longer attracted to their wives. In these cases, both individuals within a partnership may find themselves taken in a different direction. There is a lack of love between the partners in this sense; they may find themselves treated as toys rather than individuals within an intimate relationship. Because of this, there is a lack of emotional and sexual rejection from their partner. Moreover, each member of the relationship finds that they are treated as a less valuable individual. Some individuals are selfish and only think about themselves in terms of the relationship. This may be due to a variety of factors, such as a violent past, causing an individual to feel less attached towards their partner due to past experiences. Other individuals may have suffered rejection, abuse, or manipulation in their past relationships, preventing them from knowing how to behave properly within a healthy relationship. Others still may suffer from excess stress, due to changes in their life, low self-esteem, and coping issues. All of these elements may prevent healthy behaviors within a relationship. Not everyone is perfect, and in these cases there is no single individual to blame. It is important for both members of a relationship to be kind to each other, remain truthful and open, and pay each other with the respect that they are due. One should never toy with their partner's emotions; it is important to treat others with the respect that you wish to be given.

## Addictive behaviors

Addictive behaviors may begin with an obsession. An individual may find themselves spending time and energy focusing on obtaining their substance of choice. Individuals who participate in substance abuse may act alone or even secretly. Others may practice substance abuse in a collective manner, with friends or even strangers in many cases. Some individuals may suffer through a stage of denial, or the refusal to acknowledge the fact that they have an issue with their addiction. In many instances, an addicted individual commonly feels the need to use drugs in order to handle their personal problems. However, substance abuse is merely a temporary relief from the realities of everyday. In other cases, an individual may feel that they are able to escape from their troubles through substance abuse.

The majority of individuals who suffer from substance abuse are addicted to drugs or alcohol. A large amount of people are addicted to smoking cigarettes or cigars. In many cases, the individual feels that they will feel physically or mentally better if they take drugs or drink alcohol.

However, in cases when an individual takes large doses of alcohol, it is considered alcoholism. A person in this situation may drink large amounts of alcohol within a short period of time, as a way to escape from their reality by being drunk or high. Even more dangerously, individuals may operate a vehicle while drunk or high, causing a traffic accident that may result in more than one death. In this same vein, many individuals come to have issues with the law, being arrested due to their substance abuse. Without realizing what they are doing, an individual may also suffer financial difficulties due to their addiction to expensive substances, resulting in even more difficulties in their daily life. For example, an individual who smokes cigarettes will purchase a packet of twenty cigarettes, costing them $11. This results in a monthly cost of about $330, and a yearly cost of $3,960 on cigarettes alone. By quitting this addiction, an individual can save almost $4000 in a year, allowing them to save the money for more important endeavors, such as paying off debt or a mortgage.

Other individuals may find themselves behaving differently in front of their partner or their families as a result of their abuse. Statistically, males are found to take more drugs than females of the same background. This is due oftentimes to genetics and family history; when there is an ancestor who suffered from addiction in the past, later members of the family run a high risk of developing one themselves. Alcoholics, for example, are more likely to have a blood relative who is also dependent. For smokers, smoking cigarettes increases the risk of influencing family members to smoke, whether psychologically or through second-hand smoke addictions. Those who suffer from mental illness are at an increased risk of becoming addicted to nicotine, alcohol, and other drugs. It is always in your best interests to avoid harmful and addictive substances, and maintain a limit on recreational substances such as alcohol. After all, it is your life and your health that you are risking.

## Lying

Lying to your partner or to your family members can create tension in your life. It is best to avoid lying, as it is rarely beneficial and can cause lasting damage in your life and relationships. This can seriously affect your well-being. In many cases, people find themselves unable to cease dishonest behaviours; they lie to live, they lie to pass the time, and they lie to their family, coworkers, and friends. This has negative impacts on the happiness and self-esteem of both the individual and their relationship. Lying decreases, the amount of trust between you and your loved ones or your peers, therefore, it is highly important to be able to prove and show that you are trustworthy, as trust is an important element that can lead you far in life. People will come to appreciate and trust you more if they can be certain that you are a reliable and honest individual. As the famous proverb states: Honesty is the best policy. It is important to maintain a high level of honesty; you will find at the end of the day that as a result of your honesty, you now have increased self-esteem and self-confidence. Telling the truth is brave, and lying is often the cowardly path. Lying can hurt people's feelings, resulting in a loss of trust and faith between you. You will find that telling the truth will result in reduced stress levels, allowing you to feel more calm and relaxed. Although maintaining honesty can, at times, become difficult, avoiding lies will lead you to become a happier, healthier, and more satisfied individual.

In many cases, excessive lying can result in large issues. When you begin lying, you will find that it is not easy to stop the lies. If you find that you cannot control your impulsive lying, you should seek professional help; excessive lying can result in internal conflict, and the doubt of your own abilities. Many individuals become angry because they got caught lying, whether to their partner, coworkers, or even supervisors or bosses. These issues will cause more conflict in the long run and create conflict within the self.

Telling the truth is seen as courageous; while it may seem as if you have saved yourself from trouble after lying, it is rarely the case. Oftentimes it results in negative feelings between yourself and your surroundings. In fact, lying does the opposite of solving a problem, and in many cases telling the truth is the simplest way to end a conflict. Telling someone a lie and telling another individual the truth causes confusion and conflict, resulting in a constant cycle of lying, hiding, and secrecy. It is important to carefully choose the information that you wish to divulge with others; after all, it is your reputation that is at stake. Almost everyone at one time or another has told a lie – it's time to tell the truth now!

## Lack of appreciation

One reasons why a relationship between a couple may fail is due to a lack of mutual appreciation. When either a wife or a husband fails to appreciate the good that their other half does, it results in resentment and negative feelings. Both man and woman within a relationship have responsibilities; in some cases, the man may work while the woman stays home. In other instances, both may work. However, when only one partner works, the other may be unable to appreciate the hard work that goes in to earning money. Some individuals may express their resentment through the creation of unnecessary drama in order to get something out of the relationship. Others will criticize their partner until the partner feels ashamed of their actions, or put their partner down by comparing them to others. If you find that your partner is lacking in appreciation for what you do, it may be time to communicate your feelings and work to find a solution for the negative behaviours. Many individuals are toxic and enjoy making their partner feel unworthy or negative; it is important that you appreciate yourself and all that you do, and do not let others walk all over you. If you feel obliged to do something, for example, making a meal, do it for yourself as well. If you buy something thoughtful for your partner, buy something thoughtful for yourself as well. When you think about others, it is important to think about yourself. Don't worry, you won't be seen as selfish. If your partner does not think about you in positive ways, it is important to do it for yourself. If there is no one there to help you, you must stand up for your right and get things done yourself. If you find yourself feeling unworthy of appreciation, address it. It is important to feel respected, loved, and appreciated. Be strong and responsible, and you will see many changes within you. In time, you will find that your relationship is heading in a better direction.

## Broken trust

The longer you allow yourself to live within a lie, the deeper and more troublesome the damage will be within your relationship. Therefore, it is important to acknowledge your action to your partner before the discover the truth about you themselves. The longer that you hide your actions or secrets, the more they will resent you. You may not always get what you want from your partner; be honest. It is important to have a zero-tolerance policy towards dishonesty in your relationship, as all successful relationships start with a strong level of honesty and communication. You will find that you have a longer and more lasting level of commitment with your partner. It is important to build a strong foundation; it may take a lot of time and strength. It is important to give your partner time to build that strength. Acknowledge the questions that your partner asks you, avoid becoming defensive or responding to your partner with negativity as he or she may require more time in order to feel open with you. You are the only one who can answer their questions, so answer freely and do your best. It is always important to acknowledge your partner's feelings; you do not need to analyze, judge, evaluate, or find any reason to disregard their feelings. It is important that you listen and agree with them without disputing and ignoring their point of view. It takes less time and energy to allow them to express and explain their feelings. Simply follow along with the conversation; a simple method to winning trust is to be patient. Reassure your partner by allowing them ample time to rebuild trust. In the meantime, take responsibility for your actions. Respect the truth and acknowledge what you have done by avoiding excuses, rationalizations, explanations and justification towards your negative behaviours. Keep your word to do good; when trust is broken, it takes time to rebuild.

## Boredom

You should not blame yourself or feel guilty about getting bored with your relationship. Rather, it is important to analyze and understand the reason as to why you are losing interest with your partner. Do what you need to do to overcome it; many couples have been in relationships for many years, while others are new. Those who have built their relationship over a period of time are able to find ways to avoid losing interest in their partner, while those who are new to relationships may feel overwhelmed or disheartened. Some individuals are simply bored because they are not creative or lack the patience in maintaining the ins and outs of a relationship over a long period of time.

Oftentimes people find themselves becoming bored due to the daily routine. It is normal to find that your relationship is reaching a stage of stagnancy, but it is equally important to find ways to rekindle the interest within the relationship. For some, being in love may prove to become monotonous. However, this is what relationships are all about; it is important to continue loving your partner and maintain commitment.

Others may no longer feel excitement in their relationship. If this is the case, it is important to open up to your partner. You may simply need to go on a vacation or try a new place to have dinner. Doing things that bring about change and excitement in a relationship is healthy and will help maintain a relationship in the long term. In some cases, a relationship may prove to be too fragile. To avoid this, it is important not to rush into serious relationships too quickly and to take your time before dating someone. Avoid becoming the rebound or the friend with benefits. When we are bored, we may seek better opportunities. Though it is important to first focus on repairing your own relationship, at a certain point you may feel that you deserve better. If this is the case, seek better. However, while many may say that something is better than nothing it is important to know yourself and your emotional state. Avoid falling into emotional affairs with friends and colleagues at work; let these relationships be purely professional. While repairing your current relationship, it is best not to open up about your difficulties with others. Do not forget the special memories with your partner, as they will always be special in your relationship. When you reflect on your relationship, you will recall these memories.

Communication is an important key in avoiding boredom. If you feel that you tried everything in explaining your feelings to your partner, you may merely need to spend some quality time with them to make the point clear. The most successful couples maintain healthy communication. Learn your limits; spending a lot of time together may be good for some couples, but for others it may be catastrophic. It is important to balance your time and happiness within a relationship. Give time where time is due.

## No affection

We all want to be loved, cared for, and cherished by someone that is meaningful to us, but how often do we show that we do not care about others or our loved ones? You may not be the cause of this, but chances are you want to be able to receive more attention and to feel more love. People often forget to give love yet wish to receive it; how often do loved ones reach out to you to tell you about any personal problems they may have, such as behavioral problems, loss of a loved one, traumas, bad relationship experiences, abuse, living a challenging life, and family problems?

These people know that they cannot give you love but wish only to receive it. They may show frozen emotion depending the experience, and later you may realize that they cannot show you affection or pay attention to you. It is only when you ask them a question that you will find out about their situation. Some people are good at knowing when to show attention at the beginning of a relationship, others will act when everything is over and at that point they will come to show you that they were there since the beginning.

Obviously, in this scenario they are not the only one that struggling, it is you who needs affection and you are not getting it. Some people do not want to open up because they are afraid of what will happen when you find out about their problems. When you see the that relationship is declining you may think that your partner may not change over time, even if you try to open up and try to fix the problems between yourselves. Therefore, you should continue doing only your part and allow others to do theirs; do not spend too much time on people who do not want to give you affection. It's not difficult to find people who understand you and who want to be with you. However, miracles do not happen overnight, you have to do your part; start a conversation and find someone who will appreciate you and love you for who you are. Never look back or blame yourself for something that was out of your control or that you did not deserve. Share mutual respect, greet them, and move on.

Some may say that their partner won't show any affection. Another individual may say that their partner *has* no affection, no emotion, and is brutal and cold. Others may break up with their partners as an excuse for not showing enough affection. Your husband, wife, boyfriend, girlfriend, family members, friends, or even strangers may show you affection but even then, others may not regardless of whether or not you show them the same respect. Some people are born like that, though others are more reasonable. There will always be a limit and, if you cross over that limit, you may lose the bearings on your relationship. Try to balance things as much as possible; measure the relationship dynamic and as long as you feel affection and you wish to show it yourself, give affection.

## Rejection

Most mentally strong people acknowledge their emotions; if you can challenge yourself when you were embarrassed, discouraged, sad, or even disappointed, you will be able to face rejection when the time comes. When one is able to juggle and balance their emotions, he or she will be able to feel confident and deal with uncomfortable emotions in any situation.

The best way to feel healthy is to deal with coping with discomforting emotional states, as many times, when facing rejection, people may find it necessary to try to minimize the pain by convincing themselves to avoid feeling pain or feeling rejected.

There are various ways in which one can be experience rejection, either by a loved one, their family members, friends, coworkers, or even by strangers. It is important to always attempt to overcome the rejection, and find ways to stimulate your mind and your heart. Find a coping mechanism in order to avoid being hurt or offended. As you question others, question yourself in order to find answers. If you cannot find answers then you are sharing a clod relationship with your chosen one. However, some questions may not have readily available answers. Some may say that there is always an answer for any given question, but this depends on which ground you are in. You will never know your strengths until trouble comes to you, and one way of discovering your strengths is to experience rejection. As the popular proverb states, "experience is the father of wisdom." You will soon learn how to handle any typical situation after you analyze your experiences. Learn to treat people with compassion; if they respond to you with negativity, be nice and gentle and show them that you are a kind and compassionate person. Between couples, interactions can sometimes turn into a series of mind games. If you truly are for someone, you may find yourself becoming trapped in the mind games. While it's not always possible to avoid these games, you can learn how to play them and master them. In this way, you won't feel that you are in the wrong if at any point one wishes to reject you in any way.

After being rejected, ask yourself: what did I learn from it? Others can also learn from rejection. The most important thing is to be able to tolerate your pain; if you can control rejection, you will grow stronger and learn to become a better man or woman. Use rejection to gain more maturity, to mover forward as an opportunity in gaining more wisdom. Nowadays, people are mostly rejected in the world of online and application-based dating sites, where you have get rejected by hundred to get a few responses. If you can manage that type of situation, you will soon learn to manage your emotions in more day-to-day situations.

## An obstinate spouse

What can you do when you have an obstinate spouse one might ask? Usually, an obstinate spouse is created when your spouse moves out and refused to tell you where he or she lives. In this scenario, they have decided to threaten you to with the idea of cutting all contact. They will purposely to ignore your phone calls, ignore all of your voice mail messages, refuse to answer your emails, and overall he or she will be emotionally cold with you, doing everything to piss you off. He is being a jerk with you or she is being a bitch with you. He is in the mood of jerking off in front of you or she is ready to bitch at you.

You will face different attitudes with your obstinate spouse. He or she may become a party animal, in order to avoid being home as much as possible. They will go out when ever they want to with friends, and come home at night by 3 or 4 o'clock. This is a sign that your partner has behavioral issues with you. One moment they may have a different face and suddenly they change face over time. They may become very cold; your partner may be stubborn; therefore, it is necessary to find an approach in order to be able to resolve the conflict. Sometimes, based on certain situation, people have no choice but to be stubborn. It may come as a surprise if they are not normally like that, if naturally they are very free and open minded. If you can find out the problem behind their actions, you will find it easier to make the right choices. Try to understand the logic behind your spouse's decision. There is no need to argue or yell at someone who will not listen to you. Some may enjoy making people mad and angry. If you disagree with your spouse, it is important to tell them that you still care for them and are willing to continue loving them; you are ready to support her or him. Sometimes, you may lose something to win something else; use a positive approach. Avoid violence, misunderstandings, verbal or physical fighting, or freaking them out just because you are pissed off. Be patient with your loved one, learning to control your spouse can be challenging, even if he or she is narrow minded, patience bring virtue. Your wealth is your spouse when you have one. When you do not have one, he or she has no value. Put a price on him or her, over time you can replace it with something else or someone else. Your positive approach is to love and understand them.

## Hatred

Why might one come to feel hate towards their partner? Some individuals may simply not see themselves with their partners anymore; they are no longer interested in resolving or even acknowledging conflict with their partner, and they no longer can imagine their future with their partner. If you are someone who is going through a rough time, if you are highly sensitive, suffer from anxiety, or feel depressed, you may feel even more hopeless in your relationship. If you have convinced yourself that your partner should be making you happy, and they aren't doing it, you may become angry. During your time with your partner, you may no longer feel like yourself; you may feel as if your partner is hiding something from you, or not being his or herself in turn. This will make you feel even more hopeless, especially when your relationship falls short of your expectations. Being with your loved one should not make you feel any more anxious; you should not have to worry about receiving a quick and negative response to everything that you say, or spend more time arguing with him or her than having peaceful and pleasant discussions. The more you interact with your partner, the more conflict can be created, until soon you no longer wish to see them at all.

If this is the case, your partner or spouse may soon lose interest in sex, and have more negative moods, lower empathy and patience, and less interest in the things they used to share with you. This will obviously come as a blow; if you no longer view your partner through the same eyes, you will find that you have come to punish both yourself and your partner, if not your children as well. In some cases, opposites may attract, but they can later come to repel us, especially when they get in the way of sharing love and building a stronger relationship. While it's easy to blame someone else and point your finger at your partner, it is important to remember that a relationship is a two-way street. Some instances of negative relationship events include: nagging, belittling, flirting with individuals outside of the relationship, cheating, or refusing to have sex. In this case, the best action is to communicate; it is important to discuss your problems patiently and openly. It is important to accept your partner for who they are, but also to accept yourself.

# Hurt

When you feel hurt, calm down your emotions and find out what has created your pain. What exactly happened? Analyze your feelings of hurt, find solution, make decision, and appreciate the action that has happened. Put all your energy towards remaining powerful; it is important to let go your past hurtful experiences in order to heal. Do not think of negative actions and information - let the negative memory leave you.

Usually, you may find yourself feeling hurt because of the actions of another individual, or a bad situation that you found yourself in; regardless, your feelings are hurt. This may be because of a misunderstanding or miscommunication, or simply because of something negative that has been said about you. However, it is important to analyze your response; have you overreacted due to a lack of attention? Where you rejected, let down, betrayed, disrespected, criticized, or unfairly accused? In many cases, comments or criticisms from the people close to us may hurt the most. We feel a craving for love and attention from others and may feel hurt when someone attacks us and makes us feel bad. If you find yourself in a negative situation, we consider ourselves to be the victims, with the actions, opinions, and reactions of other people being considered direct personal attacks intended to hurt us.

In order to understand the underlying cause of this hurt, it is important to ask yourself what has actually happened – why are you feeling this why? You must analyze your response based on how you are currently feeling, and observe your initial reactions to the situation. Asking these questions will lead you to clearer answers, and the true cause of your emotions. In many cases, emotions may stem from beyond the event, in which case you must heal from past negative experiences and move on.

Feeling pain has no time frame; someone may feel hurt for a longer time than another individual. Will there be an ending? This varies among individual experiences. In some cases, it is a culmination of events that makes the situation severe and very painful. It is also important to analyze the intentions of the offending party; why did they say these things to you, what were they trying to do? Whether or not the offense was intentional may make a big difference in how you handle the situation, as oftentimes things are misunderstandings. Try to process the information, settle the situation, and move forward. There are different approaches to take; self reflection, asking insightful questions, and cultivating self-confidence are all important aspects to managing hurtful situations. Do not jump to conclusions without finding answers. In order to end the negative impact, focus by letting go the past feelings. Try to smile more. Try to be gracious and assertive. Focus on your strong qualities. Cultivate your self-confidence, your belief and acceptance. To better focus on your relationship with others or your loved one, let go and move words and hate from your mind. Feel better be better, forget about past and stand up in present moment and navigate for a better future. No need to blame others, no need to take words or actions personally. Accept, acknowledge and overcome hurt.

## Betrayal

Betrayal can stem from drastic mood swings. You or your partner may have different behaviors. Not knowing what to do or how to think, one may feel more depressed, while others are extremely anxious and isolate themselves. Many people have issues with nightmares, other may not be able to sleep well. When knowing that your partner betrayed you, you my have rage or feel that you need to plot revenge, some people even begin having fantasies with other people. A few percentages may become verbally and physically violent. One may become obsessed by thinking of betrayal and may lose interest on everyday activities. Some may be influence by having compulsive substance abuse such as; using alcohol, drugs or even smoking more cigarettes. Others have behavioral issues that take the form of excessive shopping, addictive gambling, and compulsive eating. Most of people think that their symptoms may go away but this is not always the case. When knowing that one has been betrayed, he or she may be influenced to become the detective; attempting to find the evidence by looking in computers, phones, cellular, wallets, credit card bill or even emails. Some may try other types of approaches to detect and find evidence. It is very emotional knowing that a loved one has betrayed you. If you seek public help or post on social media to get support and start discussing about your partner it might create more problems. This can create an aggressive behavior which can damage not only your partner but also your kids and other family members. Ask yourselves what is reasonable between you and your partner. By discussing with your partner the problems and possible solutions, you and your spouse may find ways to heal and feel less of the pain of betrayal and reestablish your relationship's trust. If you want to forget about betrayal, one way to start is to start making more love to your spouse, cooking something that he or she like the most, dressing well or even dressing sexy for him or her. Find time to make one feel more romantic and be more sexually active. Remember, cheating is not a solution but it is away to break boundaries. When you cheat you cheat within yourself and your partner. If you spouse is serious of keeping your relationship with him or her, will try to fulfill all conditions. After betrayal can you trust your spouse again one might ask? Well hopefully it won't happen gain. Usually it might take a few months to year to reestablish trust between you and your partner. When you feel that you have built a strong relationship again, you will feel ready to love him or her again.

## Secrecy

Keeping secrets has its advantages and disadvantages. When you need to keep things secret from your spouse one should ask questions about the motive behind it. Usually, a man or a woman may be having problems at job or even finding themselves unable to pay his or her bills. You should not hide anything when something is going wrong at work or if you have problem paying your bills. This may escalate stress between you and your spouse. You should not lend money to your friends or even your family members without letting your partner know. If you and your partner share and have the same bank account, then you should tell your spouse where the money is going. Moreover, if you have an illness you should tell your partner because he or she is the only who can support you in this crucial time. It is not healthy to meet with your family members in secret; you should not hide it from your partner if you meet with your siblings or parents. After all, they're are part of your family. Do not lie about spending money; if your partner has doubts about it, show her or him the receipt. If you have to take drugs do it in front of your loved one or let them know about it. If you love them, let them know. There is no need to keep an addiction or substance abuse habits hidden. Also if you have affair, one day your spouse may find out. It is really hard to have afire with one in the same time being with your partner. It is not recommended to cheat or have affairs secretly. This can create tension and break your relationship. You partner may discover if you keep a secret especially at bed time. Others, may discover it when you are drunk, or you may reveal it when you are too stressed out or during periods of grumpiness. Oftentimes, secrecy is revealed when you and your spouse are angry or either of you are tired or ill, or sometimes, when your spouse is dealing with bad news. These are the difficult issues with your spouse that you can have during hardships.

## Jealousy

Jealousy in a couple is never good, as it can create hardships. It is away of having a hidden insecurity or fear of losing someone. It is a way to control a person or to try to own him or her. However, it is normal in the human species to be jealous, even though it can be very painful and difficult. Jealously happens between siblings, family members, in friendships, at work between coworkers, and between couples. Small amounts of jealousy can be seen as ok but in the long run it can damage a healthy relationship and make it worse between couples who suffer from problems.

There are various ways of being jealous: one can fear losing someone that we care about or love, others may feel jealous due to insecurities. Another cause is when you may feel rejected and you need to be loved or receive attention. Some fear to be alone and to be left alone. We often feel jealous when our sense that a cherished connection with our loved one or other people that we care about the most are threatened. We feel that we are about to lose the person the we usually admire or like to spend time with. We feel the need to keep that person within us or with us. When we feel that our companionship, trust, growth, acceptance, mutual respect is threatened we feel jealous. We may create scenarios or situations to keep that person near us or with us. Too much jealously is never too healthy. When being jealous we often feel the need to make horrible mistakes or fee the loss of healthy real love with our partner. Some may try to put a trap between friends or loved ones to manipulate that person. In romantic relationships one should manage your emotions healthfully. One should seek support, and attempt to accept and recognize your jealousy. One should learn from your jealousy and let go of all frustration and negative emotions. Always remember yourself; your positive traits and positive memories with that person by assessing yourself. Some believe that in a relationship being jealous can be good as it helps one to care for that person. If one believes that he or she does not like him or her, being jealous is a sign of love. One may ask how to deal with jealous people? First of all, one should set boundaries. Some may change their routines so that they do not have to cross paths, others may reduce negative interactions with that person. One should ignore jealous comments by avoiding taking it personally. What is behind jealously one might ask? Usually, people are paranoid because of insecurity, criticisms, shame, and blame. They are afraid of something that has been done and that their partner may find out. They are scared of the criticisms of other people; what others might think or do. They feel shame due to their actions. In order to hide it, they create situations which lead to jealousy. You may ask how one feels when being jealous. From experience, you may feel different at one moment, it is like wind heating your face like a wave. It is mix of many different emotions such as shame and anger at the same time; it may come and go. Some may feel envious of something, others may feel sadness and resentment. You may feel inferior to your partner or someone else. You should not feel envy; try to forgive envy and accept envy by turning it into appreciation. Try to use envy to bring about positive goals. Stop judging yourself so harshly. Jealousy is also an emotion, and must be accepted as such.

## Religion

When discussing religion within a couple we often talk about being a peacemaker, and respecting the wishes of other people - including your spouse. Always avoiding conflict and focusing on loving others. A religious person may have faith but in many cases this faith tends to be the same as what your parents and siblings believe in; it is something that is passed from one generation to the other. The beliefs that your parents passed you, you will pass on to your children. It is in reality what your family believe in and seen in majority of the population. If you come from a Christian family, most likely you will believe in the prophet Jesus Christ. If you come from a Muslim family, you will end up believing in the prophet Mohammad. However, a certain type of people will ask questions or lose faith due to a variety of reasons and may come to change his or her religion. Hence, some may choose not to believe in any religion or simply identify as an atheist – a person who disbelieves or lacks belief in the existence of God or gods. Withstanding, a male or female may change his or her religious beliefs before getting married or choose to follow his or her partner or spouse in their beliefs. Some convert religion just to be with their partner. Is this true belief or it is fake? If your partner does not accept your religion, then he or she may not accept you as a part of his or her life. It is great to sacrifice but if you choose to do this, you have decided to erase your beliefs just to please your partner. Obviously, you should think about your children; what will he or she believe in from birth to adult life until death? It is your values that your children will believe in; what you will teach your children, they will learn from you. If you teach your children your spouse's religion but not yours, then your children will believe not your religion, but your spouse's. If you teach them to understand both religions, for example, yours and your partner's, they will try to understand both religions, yours and your partner's both. Then when they understand the value, they in turn will be capable of deciding for themselves. From birth, children are brainwashed with our beliefs, not theirs. When they ask questions, it is important to teach them and let them make their own choice. If you see by yourself, you will see that most and most couple married between two different culture and religion believe. Marriage between two different area of country is becoming more and more common. By observing your peers, you will realize that in certain faith combinations they are more likely to divorce. Not sharing the same beliefs can make life difficult and children handicapped. In most countries, women teach their children to believe in what they believe in due to the fact that women are most likely to be charge of their family while the men are at work. In certain situations, men also take responsibility for teaching their children about that they believe in. The older you get, the more you will mature, and the more likely you will be to marry someone who will not have the same beliefs in religion. This is becoming more and more common in the modern age. Mostly likely, what your parents passed on to you, you will pass on to your children and they will pass on to theirs.

## Parenting

It is important to understand from the beginning that happy parents most often result in happy children – this is what parenting is all about. The more time you spend with your children, the more that you will note the positive results of your attention. Sometimes, however, you may find that you are not paying enough attention to your spouse due to the attention that you are giving your children. In this case, it is important to balance the time between spouse and children. This does not mean that you should cease conversation with your loved one just to spend time with your children; your children may do many things that require your undivided attention, but this does not mean you should indulge them every time. Your spouse may also require your attention, and it is just as important that you make time for him or her. Sometimes, your partner may feel alone because you are giving too much attention to your children, or focusing all of your time on parenting alone. Remember that neither of you have experience and may not know how to handle the situation or the pressure. Sometimes, this may create a gap between both members of the couple; do not fall for it. Take the time that you require, ask your parents for help, and ask for advice if you find that you need it. You can also instruct yourself by reading books, magazines, newspapers or articles about parenting. You will find many things that can help you to become a better parent. In the early phase, parents usually have very few moments to sleep; taking care of the children is what your day is all about. Not knowing how to do it or who should be responsible for which tasks is an important thing to address.

Parenting can be difficult, but over time it usually gets easier. As you begin seeing your children growing you will feel good about your and your family's success. In most couples, when there is a new baby, no one is getting any sleep, no one getting any sex, and no one is happy. Both members of the couple may go through difficult times. Being a parent is not easy; a new baby means new parents, with a whole new to-do list for the mom or the dad. That is all about life. It is a certain that you generate one generation to the next one. It continues over and over - there will always be more to do. By being a new mother or father, you will always have more to fight about it; some reasons including money, sex, or even responsibility. There will always be something for a couple to fight about. Between you and your spouse, there will always be different parenting styles; the way you will raise them, they way they will grow up. Children will try to follow your styles. Obviously, however, with age they will develop a unique way to live.

## Separation

In some cases, you may find that you have suffered enough and decide to separate from your spouse. Even if you have tried your best, things may not always seem to work out. A legal separation may be requested through a court order. By staying separated, however, a couple is still considered to be legally married, depending on the area you reside in. You may not need to file for separation in some cases, as the law may not require you to live with your spouse. You may, however, still require a court order in order to maintain custody or visitation rights with your child. Most likely, you will require some space in order to evaluate your issues with your spouse while still maintaining your marital status.

Usually, separation occurs when partners have ceased living together. A few reasons why a couple may decide to separate includes: allowing each other time to analyze their marriage, time to gain more knowledge about their self or relationship, or if the couple is in the process of getting a divorce. It is important to understand the consequences of living alone, however. You must keep in mind how much time you will get to spend with your children should you wish to live apart from your spouse, or how much you will be required to pay in child support. Even more importantly, whether or not you or your spouse are required by law to support one another, and how you will go about dividing the property.

Furthermore, should you choose to remarry, you must wait until the separation process in your current marriage is complete. You may choose to oblige in assisting your spouse while in the separation process, taking responsibility for their debts and other financial burdens.

Separation is very difficult for children to process and understand, therefore you should think about them when making any decisions. Just as you suffer, so do your children. However, it is important not to make decisions solely due to your children; if you are suffering in a relationship, it will affect them either way, so it's best to first work on your happiness. If you cannot give them attention, affection and love then your children then perhaps you should decide to allow your spouse custody. With time it is possible for you to provide love and affection to your children even without a spouse.

## Threat of Divorce

When things don't seem to be going your way, it may seem as if everything in the world is going wrong. Usually, most of the negative actions start from your own house. As an example, your spouse may threaten you to file for divorce. This can be very disappointing; just the fact that your partner said that he or she does not want to be with you or live with you can be very painful. It is not easy to sleep in the same bed while knowing that he or she asked to divorce or is in process of letting you go. Either one has found someone else or for money reasons one wants to let you go or for some personal reason he or she decided to live apart. What will happen to your children one might ask? It is very problematic to know that your children will have to go through a difficult situation and process. When one blames you for not fulfilling her or his desire, not sharing enough of what there is to share, not valuing what he or she has done for you. It seems that love has many faces; you were so happy and suddenly you end up in sorrow. Losing your loved one can be very difficult. Arguments among married people are normal and can get pretty heated, but what happens when the person who you cared and married to constantly resorts to threatening divorce? It may become a nightmare to live with him or her. The emotional damage that one has created over time can certainly destroy a marriage. Even more importantly, the fact that someone is constantly threatening is unhealthy and unfaithful. It can damage not only the emotion aspect of your relationship, but might create even further problems. In most cases, a man or a woman may threaten their partner by saying that one wants to divorce instead of saying "shut-up". You do not need to say these things if you continue with the conversation. Hence, it is better you say "shut-up. Saying "shut-up" can often be a better option than just saying "I will end up divorcing you." Usually, between couples, when people are unhappy in marriage they displace their feelings on the other person. For example, when one is cheating, they often accuse the partner of cheating as well. Some may plan ahead by putting words in your brain and mind. When an individual want to divorce he or she will create scenario or situation so that you can blame them or even blame yourself by asking for divorce, simply saying "I am not happy". It is unfortunate, and difficult to understand why a person wants divorce when everything seems to be ok in the relationship. It is important to consider which motive your partner has in threatening divorce or creating chaos in your house. Is he or she being manipulated by an outside force, or has someone decided to enter your spouse's life to make you feel miserable? Is it a trick from one of your friends or family members to trap your spouse or you by asking for divorce? There might be many reasons why you may ask for divorce or your spouse my ask for divorce. Sometimes, we may lose control over time and take information from the outside world which creates problems inside world. Often we may value other's opinion instead of listening your spouse or even your opinion. Hence, this will lead you into the divorce process.

## Divorce Process

Depending where you live, each individual goes through a different divorce process. Every state or country has their unique way for filing for divorce. Laws are made to be respected and divorces are made for end relationship. When one requests a divorce, the process might take weeks, months, or even years. The length of the divorce process can be due to various factors; people have to go through the reason for divorce, agree on issues arising from the divorce, and obtaining the document and evidence needed for the divorce. If there is no agreement between the couple, it will take much longer to process or to finalize the divorce. It is not easy to ask for divorce at first. When someone decides to file for divorce, he or she may have undone many things in his or her mind. One may create drama which will end in divorce. He or she may be seen negatively in front of others. Rumors may be spread in other to put his or her partner in a bad light. Children will suffer during both the process of divorce and after the divorce. Take the time if ever you have to undergone the process of divorce. Remember, choosing divorce is to wish to end any kinds of relationship with your partner. Think about the consequences before filing for divorce. If you are not happy being married, then you may be more happy after finalizing your divorce. There is no point in living in the same house if the both of you hate each other. You will express a negative image in front of your children and any others who value your relationship with your spouse. Make peace with your spouse even though for the rest of life you will continue suffering due to hate that was created while living with your partner. There will always be problems with your children if you feel hatred toward your ex partner. Often people go through psychological harassment during the process of divorce, especially when there are children involved. If this has to happen in your life, make the right decision. If you can live happily then you will raise your children happily.

## Step-family issues

Step-family issues can be very difficult at times. Mostly, one has to work out their own issues when faced with these problems. It may take a few years for the blended families to adjust. Often grandparents are there to help their children. Usually, people get help from the clergy, support groups, and some community groups to adjust with their children.

Members of the new blended family need to be strong among themselves. They have to support each other and acknowledge their differences even though there are family losses and changes. It is important to focus on fostering and strengthening new relationships between family members – parents, stepparents, stepchildren, and step-siblings. It is preferable for the parents to consider a psychiatric evaluation if they fear that their children are dealing with the losses, torn between two parents, isolated by feelings, feeling guilty or angry, or are very uncomfortable with other family members. Your child may not derive enjoyment and or does not participate in any activities such as learning, going to school, playing, being with friends and family, or even working. You should help them to better guide their emotions and help them to be more open with people. Be as kind as possible and let them understand the benefits of your new family.

Now that you have learned all of the types of possible problems with your partner, make a wise decision before letting him or her go from your life. Most of us will go through money conflicts, no sex, cheating, poor communication, anger, lack of love, additive behaviors, lying, lack of appreciation, broken trust, boredom, no affection, rejection, an obstinate spouse, hated, hurt, betrayal, secrecy, jealousy, religion, parenting, separation, threat of divorce, divorce process and step-parents' issues while being with our partners. It is a life circle and most of us will face these 25 problems in our life while dealing with a spouse. Learn how to master these problems and you will have a better and happy life with your spouse. Do not let anyone enter in your life and attempt to destroy your family. People can be cruel, and it is important to stay away from cruel people. Live your life the way you want to live, live with your loved one, husband or wife, and your children.

Advice: Talk to him or her about your problems. See a therapist. Make a conscious effort to see the good in him or her. Look at things from his side. Be honest. Remember that marriages take work. When it's time to call quits do not call it quits. Life is better when you take action.

The following 25 reasons are why you and your partner may through difficult situations. These are the main reasons why marriages may fail. These are the reasons why you may ask for divorce from your spouse. Be very careful with these reasons; use these reasons as an advantage to keep your marriage safe. The better that you can manage your problems, the better you will find yourself able to deal with and lead a happy life.

1. Money conflicts
2. No sex
3. Cheating
4. Poor communication
5. Anger
6. Lack of love
7. Additive behaviors
8. Lying
9. Lack of appreciation
10. Broken trust
11. Boredom
12. No affection
13. Rejection
14. An obstinate spouse
15. Hated
16. Hurt
17. Betrayal
18. Secrecy
19. Jealousy
20. Religion
21. Parenting
22. Separation
23. Threat of divorce
24. Divorce process
25. Step-parents' issues

## CHAPTER 6

# THERAPIST AND YOU

One should wonder…

If a therapist proposes that you have sex, or if they joke about or make light of the topic, you should excuse yourself from the session and contact the proper board or authorities. A therapist should not talk to you about their personal problems, or mention their sexual relationships with others, nor should a therapist ask about your personal sex life. Therapy sessions should also take place in appropriate settings; if, for some reason, your therapist is to show up at your house, you should ask them to reschedule and meet at a more appropriate and public place. A therapist should not touch, hug, or attempt any other types of physical contact. Furthermore, he or she should not disclose confidential information about previous clients or patients. Your therapist is not a matchmaker; they should not try to arrange meetings between patients in therapy for any reason. Your therapist should not offer you illegal drugs or alcohol, or any substance in fact. Your therapist should maintain professionalism at all times, in all aspects. This includes not asking for sensitive information, or soliciting external payments outside of the agreed upon therapy rate. Your therapist should not ask to borrow money from you – this is taking advantage of your professional relationship. Be careful not to reveal any financial information, outside of any stress-related concerns that you may have. A therapist should not be receiving any personal belongings of yours, nor any assets such as cars or external funds, as previously mentioned.

A therapist cannot punish you for any reason; if you are late, or miss an appointment, your therapist cannot threaten you with any type of negative act. Be aware that you are free to inform anyone of your participation in therapy; your therapist should not force you to keep your sessions a secret. Whether or not you trust your therapist is up to you; your therapist should not ask you to work for him or her, or to counsel them in turn. If they charge a fee, they should not require you to volunteer for them in order to pay off the fee; your insurance may cover the costs, and there are government programs that can assist you in covering costs for mental health. Furthermore, your therapist should not suggest a business partnership, or request professional assistance in any way, such as publicity or marketing. Beware of compliments; your therapist should maintain professionalism at all times. If your therapist should not cross the line between friendly and inappropriate. They should not tell you that they enjoy your personal company, or tell you that you are special. On the other hand, they should not insult you in any way during or after sessions. Your therapist should respect the therapeutic legal law and approach.

## How can psychotherapy help an individual?

When an individual seeks help, they may not know how to proceed or where to go initially. This is an appropriate time to consult a doctor, or a close family member or friend for advice and support in making this decision. Finding a counselor or another professional that can assist you in going through a difficult time is an important decision, and oftentimes a psychologist, psychiatrist, social worker, or counselor is recommended. The main reason for counseling is to understand your illness – what is actually happening to you physically, emotionally, and mentally. It is important to understand the basic issues of your health in order to better assist you with unpleasant memories and other negative side-effects. For example, when working with a psychologist, you may try to define and reach wellness goals, cope with stress, and find a variety of coping mechanisms that are attuned to your situation. You may find that you need to follow a routine in order to cope with your negative emotions, and a psychologist will assist you in creating that routine. It is important to be open with your psychologist; if you want to overcome fears and insecurities, it is vital that you tell your psychologist the issues that you are dealing with so that they may fine-tune your sessions in order to help you begin a healing process. It is necessary to identify triggers that may worsen your symptoms, such as fears and insecurities, which will only stifle progress if not brought out in the open.

However, talking to your psychologist is not the only way to open up about what is on your mind and bothering you. Sometimes, you can simply vent to someone who is close to you and important in your life. If you can maintain balance, you will be able to improve your relationships with friends and family members. Through this improvement, you will find balance and new ideas as to how to cope with crises. As a result, you will be able to establish a stable, dependable routine, and understand the particular things that upset you, and the reasons behind them, while working towards solving these issues.

Through analysis of your fears, worries, triggers, and overall issues, you can end destructive habits that are causing damage in your life, such as drinking, smoking, drugs, or unsafe sexual habits. Understanding the consequences of these habits will allow you to form and maintain healthy goals and you will find yourself feeling better physically, emotionally, and mentally, allowing you to enjoy the time spent with the people you care about the most.

## The most common triggers

The most common triggers that therapists often face in counseling are: stress, self-esteem, relationship, life transitions, depression, dependency, anxiety, anger and addictions. Psychologists can usually help with reducing your stress, guide you into forming better relationships, and help you to improve your self-esteem. Through counseling you will learn how to calm yourself, work past having addictions, and learn to control yourself by pushing away any harmful and dangerous habits such as drug use and addiction to alcohol. Counseling can also help you to understand your past, present, and future, and to put things into perspective. As a result, you may overcome mental illnesses such as anxiety and depression. Psychologist and other types of therapists will always be there to help you function better, working to help you grow in the most crucial moments.

## The most common reasons to seek a counselor:

In many instances, problems occur between couples and those who are facing break-ups or divorce. Human emotional responses to such life-altering situations often result in suffering. Sometimes, clinical depression may happen as a result, leading to severe health issues. Losing a partner is very difficult to manage, as is suddenly becoming a single parent. Sharing custody of children may simply become sorrowful and expensive for men and, unexpectedly, living alone can be also difficult. Raising children alone can be a hectic and often people realize the value of being in a couple only after leaving their partner. Others may feel better emotionally or mentally especially if their relationship with their partner was difficult or abusive, and some may suffer due to the loss of a job or other issues in their career. Maintaining a particular standard of life for years, then suddenly having to change your lifestyle as a result of losing a job may create severe financial strain and result in tension between couples and family members. Similarly, not making enough money may be difficult for many individuals, and others may choose to find a new job, only to become overwhelmed with the change.

Many people who suffer from severe pain may also suffer from depression. Some individuals may have difficulties getting out of bed, going to work, or performing basic tasks throughout their day. Lack of energy or physical ailments such as fibromyalgia or insomnia may result in a lack of motivation, pleasure in life, and overall faith. This may result in relationship strain, and cause even more suffering for the individual. Although there are many types of medications to help handle depression, it is always a good option to initially seek recovery through counseling, to avoid the side-effects and costs that may come with prescription medication. Specialist recommended activity to handle depression includes exercising, socialization, and personal therapy. Volunteering and developing a specialized interest may also facilitate the recovery process.

Many individuals may develop feelings of anxiety, panic attacks, phobias, general nervousness, or feelings of hopelessness. These are all reasons to seek consultation with a therapist or counselor. It is important to take these feelings seriously, as they may result in even more negative consequences over time, and potential for healing quickly is greater if negative emotions are acknowledged sooner. Individuals may simply be unable to cope with the stress of everyday life, resulting in unresolved anger issues and strenuous personal relationships. Learning to express your emotions will be beneficial not only to yourself, but to your personal relationships with family and friends.

It is estimated that around 50% of couples in Western society end in divorce. Oftentimes couples have difficulties in communication and raising children. New parents may find it difficult to raise their new stepchildren, causing a rift between two families. This results in sibling rivalry, custody battles, and other financial concerns, not to mention the emotional tale taken on the children in question. Through the involvement of family members in the therapy process, the healing process becomes simpler.

Many families dealing with relationship issues are oftentimes not aware of the option of professional therapy. In this case, a professional advisor may intervene, and guide the family members to the appropriate approaches in attending therapy. Oftentimes familial issues may arise through the children; the child may be bullied in school, or suffer from a learning disorder. They may become anti-social as a result, resorting to an online world rather than the outside world, through media such as texting, video games, pornography, and chat rooms. While this is a side effect of advancing technology in a modern age, it can also become a greater issue within the family if left unaddressed. Without social interaction and greater understanding between family members, children may develop health issues, mental or physical. This may in turn result in stress-related issues for their parents, who may be unable to separate work from home and as a result risk their career. In short, it is a vicious cycle.

Another common familial issue is addiction. While there are many types of addictions, some of the most common are tobacco, alcohol, drug addiction (including marijuana), and even gambling. The uncontrollable nature of addiction has many negative side-effects within a family unit. Smoking, one of the most common addictions, increases the risk of asthma and other bronchial ailments in small children and family members who become second-hand smokers by proximity.

Another addiction is alcohol; alcoholism causes a variety of issues, but one of the most common is alcohol-related violence. When a family member is under the influence, they may become emotional, agitated, and may resort to physical and emotional violence against their family members. During this state, many alcoholics report "blacking out", or being entirely unaware of their actions for a significant period of time. Oftentimes they will wake up in an unfamiliar setting, or in police custody.

Drug addiction is another common occurrence among dysfunctional families. While individual side effects depend on the particular drug that is being abused, the general effect of drug addiction is negative and widely detrimental to the user and all of their relationships. Drug abuse can cause physical illnesses – even death – mental degradation, and tension in relationships. Drug users oftentimes become violent or delusional, particularly when they are in between hits.

Finally, gambling is one of the top addictions among adults. This fixation may result in the loss of financial and other assets, including cars and houses. This results in issues between spouses, and causes a rift between family members, who are oftentimes affected by the carelessness of the addicted party.

After having lost someone, or suffering grief, extreme distress may occur and result in depression and other mental health issues. It is important in these instances to find a support group or a therapist who can work with you throughout your healing process. Communication is key; it is important not to become anti-social, but to participate in discussion with others who have experienced a situation similar to your own. Through this process, you will find suggestions and advice for honoring the loss of a loved one.

Eating disorders are another cause for physical and mental illness. Some individuals may struggle with their weight, and others may find that they are not eating simply because they do not find themselves having an appetite, oftentimes as a result of the stress of daily life. Women are the most commonly affected demographic of eating disorders; the desire to lose weight despite the reality of their physique may result in anorexia nervosa, bulimia, and other eating-related disorders. A specialized trainer may be of assistance in this case; information on how to keep in shape through healthy and safe methods will prevent eating disorders.

Another reason for attending counseling is having low, or a lack of, self-esteem. We are only human; we may sometimes not make the best impressions and can lack assertiveness, leading to isolation and unhealthy relationships. This can also affect performance in the work place. Through healthy coping mechanisms, one can learn to become more assertive and confident without becoming aggressive. Taking the initiative to seek out a counselor or therapist will allow you to discover the value of working with a mental health professional; once you have broken this boundary it becomes easier to understand the self.

Individuals who have attended therapy have appreciated the process and found it overall a useful investment. "According to Howes,.R. PhD, Psychology Today's own 2004 survey, more than 27% of all adults (an estimated 59 million people) received mental health treatment in the two years prior. Of this group, "47% report a history of medication, but no therapy; more than a third (34%) report a history of both medication and therapy; and 19% report a history of therapy, but no medication." If my math is correct, that means somewhere around 30 million adults were in psychotherapy during that two year period (2014)". That is a significant number; some individuals pay for counseling while others receive free care due to their financial situations, health systems, or their country of residence. The sooner one attends therapy, the sooner one will begin to feel the positive effects of counseling. The main goal for doctors, psychologists, therapists or counselors is to help you develop a way to understand what is going on with you and your surroundings. Professionals are there to help you; therefore, you should not be afraid to seek help.

Communication is important in all relationships; many individuals utilize therapy as a way to assist them in becoming stronger communicators. When one cannot explain something to someone or is unable to understand what the other is saying, conflicts may arise. You will find many highly qualified therapists and counselors who are skilled at helping people communicate their feelings and resolve their issues.

What happens when one cannot trust their therapist, or simply does not have the financial capabilities to finance counseling? Depending on their issue, individuals may seek assistance from friends or family members, who can provide support, information, guidance, and experience. This level of communication and support may be enough for many; experience is the father of wisdom, and oftentimes older family members may be able to provide enough advice for an individual to work on solving their own issues. If, however, your family members are unavailable or you do not wish to burden them with your issues, you may choose to rely on a close friend instead.

Usually, when one is suffering from distress, side-effects may include the inability to sleep, eat, study, socialize, or otherwise enjoy life. If you suffer from any of these symptoms, it is advisable to seek medical assistance. Therapy may be your final option, as oftentimes issues may be medical in nature.

Therapy can be seen as support in coping with grief, physical illness, the end of a relationship, career changes, or other life-altering events. It is important to allow yourself a chance to heal your body and mind, to be open minded and understanding of yourself. Through self-exploration, you may be able to determine your personal goals, career goals, relationship needs, and other life-enhancing areas.

Individuals may pursue counseling and therapy for a variety of reasons. Some may enter therapy to address major life changes, such as divorce, and others may seek help in managing mental health conditions, like depression. There's a common misconception that people who go to therapy are "crazy," when in fact, most therapy clients are ordinary people struggling with common, everyday issues. Many people seek counseling because they have identified specific goals or issues that they wish to work on. Others may be encouraged by family, friends, or medical professionals to seek help, and in some cases, a person may be mandated to attend therapy as part of a court ruling or by a parent or guardian (if the person is a minor). These are some of the issues commonly treated in therapy:

The following information was taken from the Internet especial from the site: Good Therapy.org (2017). It is alphabetically ordered and provides an overview of some problems why one should need psychotherapy.

## A
ADHD, Abortion, Abuse, Addiction, Aggression, Anger, Anxiety and anxiety

## B
Bipolar, Breakup, and Bullying

## C
Career Counselling, Child issues, Chronic Illness, Cognitive Impairment, and Communication Problems

## D
Depression, divorce, Domestic Violence and Drug

## E
Eating Disorder, Emotional Abuse, and Emotional Intelligence

## F
Family Problem, Fear, Friendship

## G
Gambling Addiction, Grief, and Guilt

## H
Health and Helplessness

**I**
Identity Issue and Isolation

**J**
Jealousy

**L**
Learning Difficulties

**M**
Men's Issues, Midlife Crisis, Money Crises, and Mood Swings

**N**
Narcissism

**O**
OCD (Obsessions and Compulsions) and ODD (Oppositional and Defiant Behavior)

**P**
Panic Attack, Paranoia, Parenting, Phobias, Physical Abuse, Posttraumatic Stress, Pregnancy Prejudice, and Psychosis

**R**
Relationship and religious

**S**
Schizophrenia, Self-Esteem, Sex Addiction, Sexual Assault, Sexuality, Sleep Disorders, Social Anxiety, Spirituality, Stress and suicide

**T**
Terminal Illness, Traumatic Brain Injury

**V**
Values Clarification

**W**
Women's issues, Work Place Issues, and worry

**Y**
Young Adult Issues

# CHAPTER 7

# DEVILS AND ANGELS: THE PSYCHOLOGY OF GOOD AND EVIL

## Introduction

We often ask ourselves why some individuals become evil - those that are manipulated and controlled by darker aspects of human nature - while others go above and beyond to be good and do good, oftentimes on a global scale. It is difficult to pinpoint any exact equation of morality, or even to discern the true nature of each individual we encounter. In many cases, concepts of good and evil are merely superficial - for example, a group of people rallying around an individual and praising them for being good and selfless would, to an outsider, make them "good". In modern terms, many would refer to this type of image-formulation as marketing or personal branding. It is a process that depends not only on how the individual wants to be perceived, but also on how others want to perceive them. An individual deemed to be a hero one day can just as easily be perceived as a criminal the next, with perceptions changing for better or worse depending on a variety of elements, both internal and external. With the introduction and popularity of social media it is even simpler for the individual to alter their public image accordingly, making it even more difficult to discern which individuals are good and which are evil, and, therefore, to be avoided. With this in mind, the concepts of good and evil become even more abstract and difficult to analyze. Cultural, philosophical, and psychological relativism require an objective and analytical eye in the face of generalizations, rationalizations, and stereotypes. Perceptions and concepts vary across culture, geography, and history - what is evil to one individual may be viewed as peaceful to another.

## Evil

Experience is key when attempting to identify good and evil, as many people do not realize until they have either experienced the good, or lived through the bad. While it would be simpler to state that those who are evil look as such - whether it be a pair of horns or a forked tongue, like the Western idealization of the devil - it is rarely, if ever, the case in reality. Further descriptions of an evil individual are found throughout literary, religious, and artistic works, and may include a thin moustache, pointed goatee, or an expressed dislike for religious figures. However, as previously stated, these are only visual elements which oftentimes fail to accurately reflect an individual's true disposition.

When referencing beings of evil, they are oftentimes associated with superhuman forms, supernatural powers, and in relation to supernatural creatures. In religious contexts, beings now known as demons, witches, spirits, and sea monsters are depicted as stylized representations of evil forces, more often than not in a metaphorical sense. Nowadays, evil is depicted within popular culture as the "supervillain", an otherwise human figure who possesses extraordinary abilities without a moral compass. In a more relevant context, evil is acknowledged through labeling - criminals are known as such, and given specific identifiers based on their crimes - murderer, rapist, abuser. While there are variations across cultures, the concept of evil is one that is consistently present across the world, often juxtaposed with the concept of good.

When discussing the supernatural, we often refer to the concept of faith in spirits and dark forces, whether they be our own beliefs or others. In this sense, when seeing an individual whose actions are so unimaginable, we often find ourselves analyzing a single action in an attempt to understand their motives. In many cases, we may find ourselves responding negatively against the individual or organization that we have deemed "evil". While we may feel ourselves justified in these actions, based on our contextual evidence and individual beliefs, when it comes to political or historical contexts, the term "evil" may be just as harmful and dangerous as the act of evil itself. When misapplied, or used without sensitivity or justification, the concept of evil - being based on abuse, vengeance, or otherwise - becomes a weapon.

For every action, there is a reaction, and one can view an evil action as the type of reaction that a mentally unbalanced individual would have against the world around them. Actions such as these may include cheating, lying, or causing harm to another individually, be it physically, mentally, or emotionally. But what is the root of these actions? While many argue that individuals who commit crimes do so as a result of deprivation - whether it be of food, cleanliness, social contact, sexual contact, wealth, or emotional interaction - others argue that criminals and evildoers are born as such, whether as a result of destiny, spiritual possession, or "bad wiring". Environment also plays a large role in the actions of individuals, particularly in the case of institutions. Depending on an individual's socioeconomic background, they may either affect or be affected by social institutions. For example, a country's leader may consider themselves to be devoted to the happiness and strength of their people. They will make any decision necessary to protect their society and the people within it, even if it means destroying a neighboring society whose existence threatens their own. In this case, thousands of people have just died to protect their nation, soldiers have died to protect their families. Was the leader acting in evil? Who is to say which lives are more valuable? Oftentimes it is a matter of perspective - those who have been saved may view their leader as great and wise, while those who have suffered loss in the neighboring country view their opposition with hate and vengeance.

## Good

In many societies, when an individual is born they are considered to have a clean slate - they are innocent, viewed as untarnished by the forces of evil. In religious contexts, children are considered to be gifts - it is a gift from God to give birth, to create a human being, and, therefore, a child is a gift from heaven. Individuals that maintain this purity as their lives go on are often considered "good", and those who are exceptionally good may come to be called Angels.

There are many types of Angels - some are visible, others are only felt through the senses of touch and hearing. Other Angels may take the form of unknown creatures in a variety of shapes and forms. According to some religions, Angels that do not appear visible to the human eye are sent to Earth by God, and still others may not be visible to those that are unworthy - whether as a result of their actions, beliefs, or behaviours. Many of these Angels will protect and defend those who are innocent and who believe.

To define an Angel, or one who is good, is just as difficult as defining an individual who is evil. One might describe an Angel as being kind, respectful, caring, and generous, etc. In other words, what makes an individual an Angel is how others perceive their behaviour - it is, in essence, a definition, which may vary among individual perceptions.

Others may view Angels as non corporeal forms, those who may temporarily take control of your body, so that they may feel the pain and hurt that you are suffering in your stead, to prevent you from suffering the same fate. This process may be viewed as evil to some, while to others it may seem generous and selfless. But who decides?

In the case of war, do Angels interfere? Who decides which individuals they will protect, and how many are there to complete this task? It is questions such as these that have concerned philosophers throughout history: why would God create evil and good in the same breath? The answers to these questions and the questions themselves are subject to great interpretation, depending on the belief system of the individual undertaking the task.

One thought system is that the perception of life as unfair is what proves that it is inherently good. For example, an Angel may protect you, but will avoid harming someone else to do so. In this sense, they are maintaining their goodness while also keeping you from too much harm. If they were to pick and choose, then life would truly be unfair.

When in doubt, the individual must take small steps in order to maintain their faith. Staying focused on the task ahead, or what their heart tells them will allow them to move forward more steadily. Throughout life, we meet many individuals who differ in style, attitude, morality, and beliefs. Who we choose to trust or mistrust is up to us, but we should not allow it to dictate our actions. There will always be people who wish to hurt you one way or another - life is too short to waste time hating anyone. Your actions will depend on your judgment.

## Agree to disagree

You don't have to win every argument - while some are necessary, others should be avoided. If someone is looking to argue with you, the best solution is to ignore them and avoid fueling the fire. Allowing them to "win" will only make you a better leader. A simple way to end a dispute is simply to smile: by using positive reinforcement, you avoid exposing yourself and causing unnecessary conflict.

## *Cry with someone*

Crying and discussing one's feelings with a trusted friend is always more cathartic than crying alone. By sharing your troubles, you are able to view yourself through the perspective of others and put your own issues into perspective. When surrounded by many people, you will be surrounded by hope and better understanding - you are not the only one who is suffering. Oftentimes, the people you share your troubles with may not stay in your life for good, but may simply share your sorrow and move on, fulfilling their presence in your life.

## *Make peace with the past...*

...so you don't screw up the present. By letting go of the things that have hurt you, you will see your life through a different angle. Through peace you will rule not only yourself, but you can guide others as well. Peace will define you - it will make you and those around you happy, leading you to the truth and to love.

## *Don't compare your life to others*

Just as people have individual triumphs, they also have individual sorrows. Before coveting what someone else has, ask yourself if you would be willing to covet *all* of their life - the good and the bad. It is impossible to know how each individual lives their life - some are stronger than others, many have pasts that define who they are today. Just as a joke may be funny to one person and offensive to another, so are individual lives - we each carry different experiences which form who we are in the present. You have no idea what their journey is all about. This is actually the beginning of the truth. Do unto others.

## *If a relationship has to be a secret, you shouldn't be in it.*

By keeping a relationship secret, you will only end up hurting yourself and your partner in the long run. People enjoy keeping certain situations in secret, but secrets never last too long: we are human and need to share our experiences. Keeping secrets may lead to future conflict, harming yourself and those around you. Treat yourself the way you want to be treated by others. If you treat yourself kindly, you will be able to respect someone else and they will respect you in return.

Some might ask what the most important part of the body is, and the answer is that it is the brain. Without the strength of the brain, the body cannot reach its full potential. For example, in many relationships, sex is a defining and important aspect of maintaining a healthy and happy connection. In many ways, the brain is the most important sex organ, as it allows you to experience your partner in many ways. Your brain also allows you to communicate with your partner. Through positive and healthy communication, such as giving your partner compliments, your relationship will grow stronger.

## *What other people think of you is none of your business.*

We often worry about how we are perceived by other people. We may feel hurt when we are judged, or commented on, or betrayed when discovering that a friend has said something unpleasant about us. On the other hand, we may feel happy upon hearing a compliment or learning new things from mass media. While it is normal to react to these situations, it is important not to take them too seriously. There are 7 billion people on the earth and not everyone will view you in the same light. Therefore, in order to receive positive reactions, we must portray ourselves in a positive light.

## *Time heals almost everything*

Give it time. When it comes to healing, everything has a time frame. What may take you years to overcome, may take months or decades for someone else. Just as a physical wound varies from person to person, so do mental and emotional wounds. Time has no beginning or end; we can only measure it through actions. When we allow ourselves time to heal, we can move forward with greater positivity.

Keeping these guidelines in mind, who can you consider an Angel in your life? For many, a doctor is an Angel, those who save lives. For others, engineers, who build and create, are considered angels. Lawyers, police officers, and psychologists, may all be considered Angels as well. While these figures all have the potential to do good, they have the equal potential to do evil. In this sense, it is their individual action that determines their morality. Hence, an Angel is who you believe they are, and for many people, that person could be you.

# CHAPTER 8

# COUNSELING

## Counseling

Many individuals who have suffered past traumas may choose to undergo professional counseling, however, there are a variety of elements to keep in mind.

### *Finding a counselor*

Many counselors hold degrees - either Master's or Doctorate - while others are simply members of a professional's association. In the case of the latter, their practice must be reviewed over the course of several years in order to confirm their qualifications. However, not all counselors are qualified to assist you with your particular set of issues, therefore it is important to familiarize yourself with a counselor before fully committing.

### *How should a counselor behave with you?*

Problems may occur with counseling when a counselor does not have enough training, or training in a specialized area, therefore it is important to keep in mind whether or not you seek a general or specialized counselor before proceeding. A counselor should clearly express whether or not they can assist you with your specific concerns, and how they intend to work with you.

A good counselor will explain the process, as well as the intended results. Counselors should make you feel comfortable and safe - you should never feel embarrassed, hurt, or judged by your counselor. Counselors will also not attempt to touch, hug, or kiss you without consent. It is important to keep in mind cultural contexts, as well as personal wishes, in situations like this. If a counselor ever makes you feel negative or uncomfortable in any way, you may contact the board or association with which the counselor is licensed in order to file a formal complaint. It is important to do so, as to prevent future individuals from being harmed by their actions.

A counselor should not blame your family, friends, partner, or children for your issues, but should allow you to distinguish right from wrong for yourself. Many counselors may wish to disclose their own experiences in order to assist you with yours - if you do not feel comfortable with this, express this. Feel free to ask questions or for clarification if needed, and if you find yourself needing assistance with something non-therapy related, you may ask for assistance or for a referral to someone who can help. However, your counselor should never disclose your personal information with anyone else - your identity should be kept private.

If you find yourself uncertain with the level of qualification that your counselor has, you may choose to give them a trial period. In this case, allow yourself to distinguish good and bad practices, in order to determine whether or not your counselor is right for you.

If you find yourself confused by the complex or medical terms used by your counselor, feel free to speak up and ask for clarification. Do not feel ashamed - your counselor is there to help you, and it is important that you are able to fully understand them. The more you understand, the better you will feel. If you feel that you should focus on a particular area, let your counselor know. If you simply need to vent to someone, you may also do that. Your counselor is there to help you heal, and how you do that is up to you.

Many counselors may focus only on feelings and somatic experiences rather than thoughts, cognitive processing, and insight. If you feel that this is not the right approach for you, speak up. Your counselor should be able to determine what is important to you, but be aware of unsolicited advice. Your decisions are your own, and your counselor should encourage, but not pressure, you into making changes or personal decisions.

Similarly, if a counselor attempts to keep you in therapy against your will, first contact the appropriate board or association in order to report their behaviour, then change counselors. While many counselors believe that their approach is best, they should not pressure you into remaining in their care. If your counselor is frequently forgetful, impersonal, inattentive or generally rude, this may be a sign that you need to change counselors - during your sessions, you are the priority.

Your counselor should be professional and sensitive towards cultural and religious differences. You should not feel threatened or insulted. If your counselor ignores or denies the importance of religious and cultural aspects of your life, you may choose to find a counselor who is more sensitive to your needs and belief system.

## *Differentiating a good therapist from a bad one*

In most areas, medical and mental health professionals must meet a specific educational and training requirement before setting up a practice. Qualified professionals must meet the basic requirements of education, training, and licensure before becoming counselors.

When choosing a counselor, take your time to verify their credentials and experience in order to determine whether or not they are right for you. At the beginning of your session, your counselor should explain the process and how you can benefit, without making empty promises or guarantees. Oftentimes, multiple sessions are required before results are seen, many individuals require years of counseling before they feel comfortable with their progress. Before each session, your counselor should prepare you for the next session, by scheduling appointments or providing you with helpful tools.

Upon beginning counseling, you may feel awkward and unsure how to proceed. Good communication with your counselor is key - by expressing your concerns, your counsellor can adjust their sessions accordingly in order to best suit your needs. Your counselor should not force you to relive traumatic experiences or pressure you into saying something against your will.

## Working as a counselor

Many people choose to pursue a career in professional counseling as they enjoy helping people and making a difference in their lives. However, counseling is an important field, and therefore must be approached with responsibility.

## Consent and other legal issues

Before beginning a session with a client, you should have their written consent to begin therapy with them. Your client must be aware of all benefits, risks, and treatment techniques before entering a counseling agreement. This is to protect both yourself and your client, should issues arise. Your client should also be fully aware of your counseling fees, as well as insurance and privacy information. It is also important to have a plan should the need to cease therapy arise.

Although a client's information should maintain confidential, if there is a danger to the client or to someone else, the counselor is allowed to speak out or seek outside assistance. However, these instances must be treated with caution on a case by case basis. It is particularly important to maintain client confidentiality amongst clients - do not, under any circumstances, use the stories of other clients as anecdotal evidence for another. Along with maintaining professional ethics, this will maintain a strong bond of trust between counselor and client.

## As a client...

### Maintaining healthy communication

One of the most important factors between client and counselor is communication. Good communication is key in successful therapy and potential recovery. Everyone has their own communication styles: it is important to express yourself to the fullest degree of your ability, in order to encourage a stronger bond of communication. It is also your counselor's responsibility to communicate clearly throughout the session and entire counseling process. This will allow for a better connection between you and your counselor.

There are several factors involved in the foundation for clear communication in therapy. The first step is for your counselor to clearly explain their counseling process by providing examples, pros and cons, and explaining how the process of therapy works. The second step to creating a healthy foundation in counseling is by creating a goal for your therapy alongside your counselor. This will allow you to have a concrete point to move towards in your sessions, and provide you with further focus. Third, when in sessions, your communication with your counselor should be natural and conversational, in order to make both parties feel more comfortable.

At some point during your process of therapy, your counselor may introduce role play into your sessions. Role play is an excellent way to allow you to better understand confusing situations. It will allow you to express negative blame or destructive issues in a safe, enclosed environment, without fear of self harm or harm to others.

Your therapist may soon be able to distinguish your symptoms, which will in turn allow you to hone a set of coping skills in order to maintain daily treatment. In distinguishing your symptoms, your counselor will be able to discern the underlying roots and causes to your illness or issue, which serve as important elements in the healing process.

## *Showing empathy in a therapeutic relationship...*

Therapists are naturally empathetic, a prime quality that allows counselor and client to build a strong relationship based on mutual trust. When both client and counselor work together, the chance of therapeutic progress is increased. A good therapist maintains a productive and professional relationship with their client at all times, as well as a respectful one. Your counselor should treat you as an equal; you should not feel inferior or put down by your counselor.

## *Recognizing progress...*

While feeling positive emotions may be a sign of recovery, it is important to remember that even if you are not recovering quickly, it does not mean that your counselor is a bad one, or that they are preventing you from recovering. Recovery time depends on the individual, and varies from person to person.

There are several ways you may notice progress in your daily life. First, you may notice emotional changes - you may find yourself feeling happier in your day to day, or calmer in situations that once upset you. You may also feel more hopeful about the future, or ready to tackle problems that you face. Progress in recovery might also allow you to form or reform bonds with those who are important to you. Your decision making processes will be altered for the better, and by extension, those around you will react positively to your positive energy.

## Psychotherapy: The Good, The Bad, and The Dangerous

While it is great to be happy everyday, it's not always a possibility for everyone; there will always be something that upsets us, whether it be hardships, loss, or stress. Many individuals suffer from verbal, sexual, and psychological abuse, while others may feel neglected or suffer from poverty or financial strain. Still others may face medical challenges, or challenges within their relationships. All of these cause distress, preventing us from reaching our full emotional potential. Luckily, psychotherapists are available to assist us in coping, living well, and healing.

### *Psychotherapy...*

A counselor is not there to simply give you advice - they are not there to be your friend or romantic partner. Counseling is a careful practice with support, protection, and boundaries. It is both an art and a science.

Many types of therapy focus on both internal and external health, including thoughts and behaviours. Through these therapies, you will be able to find a connection between your body and mind, allowing you to understand your external and internal worlds. This will allow you to communicate and make better choices. Many individuals suffer from trauma, or threatening life conditions. Through years of research, it has become more possible to distinguish issues and illnesses, allowing patients to accept change and move forward.

All types of modalities require technical skills and high sensitivity from professional counselors. Therapy has the potential to provide help or harm, therefore it is important to work with a licensed professional.

### *Characteristics of a good therapist:*

A professional therapist should hold a degree from an accredited university, as well as a certificate of practitioner training. Once in the career field, maintaining doctor-patient confidentiality is required.

Professionalism is also key: attending appointments on time, working in a professional setting, and returning phone calls in a timely manner. While in the session, communicating clearly is important, as is respect of cultural, racial, and religious differences. Proper paperwork and medical notes must be maintained and provided, and referrals to outside consultants may be provided if needed. In short, a good therapist will be emotionally and physically present, persistent, and patient.

## What to avoid:

While there are many high quality therapists out there, unprofessionalism can occur. Signs of an unprofessional or low-quality therapist include: attending sessions late without notice, or canceling appointments altogether. Insulting patients or clients, or refusing to return their calls or emails. A therapist should be attentive during your sessions: falling asleep, answering phone calls or emails, or allowing interruptions are all unprofessional behaviours. During sessions, your therapist should keep your discussions relevant and professional - no mocking, insults, or awkward and revealing personal information.

A therapist should NEVER: block you from exiting or entering the room, book appointments during late hours, bring children into your sessions, ask you on a date, kiss or touch you, scream or insult you, practice experimental treatments, offer you food, drugs, or alcohol, ask you to pay them extra money, or participate in any other behaviours or activities that make you feel uncomfortable, unsafe, or unhappy. If your therapist does any of these things, contact the legal board or association immediately.

CHAPTER 9

# ATTACK

## Attack and Therapy

What can you say when one is being attacked? Every human on earth has been attacked in one way or another at least once in their lifetime. Attack has many forms and can be committed in many ways - some voluntary, others involuntary. Since the creation of the human species we have evolved with time. If you study history, humans have been attacking other humans for various purposes.; either to rule, or to dominate, to hurt physically, some psychologically, other socially, some emotionally, and some morally or some natural disasters or even accidents. They might be many reasons why we get attacked or perhaps you saw someone being attacked or heard that people got attacked. Can you do something about this? You can change yourself by respecting everyone, however, you cannot control everyone and ask them to change the way you want. When talking about controlling we take about people with high responsibility and respect. We elect people to represent us within our country and other countries. They become our voice, they are elected as President or Prime Minister or even Chancellor or other types of titles. They are the head of a country. If you take the time to think and see your surrounding, you will see that many people have various titles and responsibility. If you are attacked you call the police, you go to the hospital to see a nurse then a doctor, you may need to talk to a lawyer or even a judge. Just through the actions of one attack you have involved 5 people with different titles. So in the following paragraph I will discuss various types of Attack in our world and the benefits of having a therapeutic session after suffering or witnessing such an attack.

When we talk about physical attacks we may be referring to soldiers who fight in war and die or even lose a part of their body. Later they are seen as handicapped and are referred to as veterans. They follow human orders, they agree to kill people and agree to die by other people. They are trained to hurt people in any way necessary. Each country spends millions of dollars to keep soldiers in their countries and to protect from invasion or other types of threats. Protecting a nation is great, to live in peace in a country is a dream nowadays. When people disagree with their political parties, this is when civil war happens. People among people hurt themselves in many ways. Some will take weapons to hurt or to kill people, other will use traps to eliminate their target party. One can use other types of forms or vehicles to hurt people. Other ways of hurting people may occur due to a variety of reasons. These individuals are known as criminals. Criminals kill people or hurt them someway in order to take advantage of others by hiding or to not get caught. Each of them might have reason to kill or even to hurt an individual physically But the real reason is often not comprehensible on a one to one basis. Think for once, you had to kill people to protect your nation and you hear noise such as machine gun or even boom exploding near you or another country use biological weapon against. The resulting memory can become a nightmare, as sometimes it is psychological. People will always feel unsafe even if there is no danger or even no threats. One of the reasons is due to various types of mental illnesses such as fear or phobia or paranoia. After war, particularly after being attacked or experiencing an attack, many soldiers need counseling or therapy. They lived a life that is unforgettable, and some may never be able to share what they experienced. Only a few words will be able to show that they suffered through counseling One may be able to express with words but may not be able to find the right words to discuss their feelings or even thoughts. Depending on the situation, the psychologists, or psychiatrists, doctors, and even therapists will have a idea of what the person in question is suffering. Hence, this will lead to understand one problems physical and mental problems.

Another way of being attacked is by having an accident. Someone may push a person and he or she fell from stairs or from something high or even pushed from the back. There are various ways and types of getting hurt witch can create and to think that one got attack. Someone may have an accident voluntary or involuntary. One may play sports and get hurt, which can be seen as voluntary, and someone else can drive a car and another car hit him or her then got hurt which can be seen as involuntary. Not every human wants to hurt other humans purposely. Sometimes we hurt people by accident other times we are cruel and hurt one purposely. Humans can be mean and it is part of various types of races and genders. Some are even racists. Those who are mean use various strategies to hurt others. Some use different types objects and other use their body to hurt people. Often one is hurt by another individual but he or she thinks that it was an accident. Many people have various way to attack another individual. You may not realize why you got hurt and how, or even who is behind this. When you think that you had an accident, you are more realistic emotionally. You may accept that you got hurt and that it was not your or even the other individual's fault. You do not think to blame someone, because you feel that it is involuntary accident. It just happens and you were in the bad place in the bad time. Hence you got hurt. Some other people may cry so much because of their pain that may think the opposite of you. One may think that he or she got hurt and finding way to pay back. Planning how to fight back in the near future can be the main intention for a person. We feel more calm when knowing that we has an accident which is no one's fault and we are very angry to know that you got hurt because it was a voluntary accident. Again, therapists may take time to follow that person in question. He or she may need physiotherapy so that the body can heel or even function the way it was before the accident. Sometimes, it is psychological, one may show syndrome or symptom depending the time and accident.

What happens when it is a natural disaster that happens in your area or city or province or states or country such as tornado, storm, earthquake, fire, flood or even heavy snow storm? It is difficult to see a big storm or even a flood destroying your house, or the roof fall because of the heavy snow weight. Often fires take place and you lose everything. Sometimes, tornadoes or earthquakes destroy your house or people's houses and you see that what you build has been gone and you have to restart from zero. Everything that you build with time was destroyed, memories erased. Some need counseling. Obviously, your counselor or therapist cannot return what you have lost over time with the natural disaster that happened to you and your people, but it will help you to heal over time as well as help you to be stronger emotionally. One will be there to hear you and to see you having tears from your crystal eyes. The psychologist will be there to support you psychologically. He or she will guide you in a better way so that you can feel release with pain that you have in your mind. Losing something valuable is difficult. For so many years we buy things and to decorate our house with our earnings is something memorable. Some may even spend a lot of money to buy toys such as expensive cars which can suffer damage with the flood. With therapy one will be able to manage the lost. We cannot blame anyone except the nature and the environment.

Socially we are attacked by people who start rumors, who gossip behind us, and who use us for their various purposes. People can be mean and can be cruel. You may have great friends but over time they may become your great enemies. Like the proverb says "keep your friends close and your enemies closer". Some reasons why your friends may turn against you can be because your may do or have something better then them. Therefore, they will try to destroy what you have. Another possibility is that you have a great career and one of your friends may dislike that and use you or try to fire you from your work. Sometimes you can have a great partner and your friends want her or him and will create damage so that he or she will leave you. This can also be called jealousy. Your child may do extremely good in school and your friends' children may not perform well, hence they will try to hurt your child to put them out of the competition. Within a few years we were fortunate to be blessed with the greatest social media networks such as Facebook, Instagram, Twitter and even YouTube and others such as Reddit and Tumblr. We can see people with a single touch of a button, but people expose themselves and expose their family, friends, and strangers. Some may put others down by showing nasty pictures and even others may copy and paste pictures to show the negative traits of a person. A few people may use software such as Photoshop or other types of software to create something through the computer or even digital camera and special effects. Some people use naked images to show others how bad you can be. Some take your face and copy and paste on another picture so that there can be a similarity. An example: "is when a male is eating and is taken a picture with the mouth open and an individual has taken your picture and decide to create pornography. Having you giving an oral sex to another male person." This can be discussing but it is often done by cruel people who are your competitor or who does nasty video to portray you negativity within your society or even other cultures. Hence, it is painful to see yourself sucking a penis of another male done by software to show pornography. If you are the targeted one, you will need counseling, this is damage your mind and hurt your feelings. This is putting spots in your name and images. Showing the world that you are poor and desperate for money and sex. It is to degrade you from top to grown. This has an effect psychologically and emotionally. People and enemies will make money by selling a video of you created in pornography. It is one way of taking a knife and back stab you. Religiously it is not acceptable. Seeing this, one will suffer and will be extremely mad on the person who did it. Obviously, those who want to expose publicly naked have no problem see themselves but those who want to be clean or even pure will struggle because of dirtiness of the society. There are over 7 billion people in this world and you need to understand that at least a few thousand will be nasty, cruel and mean towards other people just to make money behind them and use them for their purpose. Some people want to expose their fantasy. One will heal over time by not thinking about it but if you went though that be gentle with you as you know that it is to mock you and lose face and having bad reputation.

Either you want rule, or to dominate or to hurt physically, psychologically, other socially, some emotionally, and some morally or even by accident, people will always continue hurting people. There are many ways to create crime and they are various way to stop dealing with crime. As long as you are safe with your surrounding you will feel better about you and others. If you are the targeted one, then it will be a very difficult journey. Be strong, be alert, be safe, and do not fall for a trap or to trap others for no reason. When you feel healthy you will feel better morally. There will always be a certain percentage of people who will suffer and who will be the target one to be stick down. Do not let others intimidate you or harm you. Stand up for your rights. Defend yourself. Use imagination and creativity without destruction and you will win the battle. In certain situations, the pen is mightier then the sword.

## Others Attack

Moreover, you will be surprised to find that there are various other types of attack in our society. Some examples include: financial, criminal, religious, work, reputation, intellectual property, political, espionage, corporation, science, cyberspace attacks and gossiping, rumors or speculation.

# Financial

In many cases, a financial attack occurs when you own a store, corporation, an organization, or any other kind of property that has a monetary value attached to it, and you get robbed, embezzled, or even suffer physical theft. Other types of attack can occur when an individual or a group of people obtain access to your bank account and withdraws money from your account without your permission. We used to see people being a pickpocketed, but now with modern technology there are more advanced and silent ways of stealing money. What is even worse is when *you* are blamed for taking money or valuable things from stores or even your company or organization; people blaming you for being a thief and stating that you have taken something without their permission. However, what is even worst is when people begin spreading false rumors about you to others. In some situations, it can be people who you know – such as colleagues, friends, or even outside people who want to work at your place and take your title or just feel the need to give you a hard time financially and mentally. Some people will tell false information to your boss or even your colleagues will tell lies abut you so that you get fired. These people are just mean. If you do your best, your boss may keep you, but with many complaints there is a chance of getting fired. As a reaction to this injustice, you may become frustrated and disappointed. We all have to work in order to continue making money and paying for our way of life and our belongings. Work is what gives us a status, keeps us busy, and makes us feel good at the end of the day. When getting paid we are happy to get paid; it is very difficult to live a life without having a salary or some stable source of money. In some countries, the government is able to help people through welfare programs that are able to provide financial assistance to those who are unable to get any kinds of jobs due to a variety of reasons including disability, unexpected unemployment, and homelessness. That is all part of program funded by taxpayers in order to help the less fortunate get back on their feet and survive in the meantime. The more we advance economically, the more there will be financial attacks and the more we will learn to detect new types of attacks and prevent them.

# Criminal

Criminals are everywhere in this world; you will hear about them, you might see them, they might be near you. Some are easy to detect, while others are very hard to find or notice. Some functions are invisible to detect with your eyes. In certain situations, there are various types of criminals and some function with a large group of people, or are part of a criminal organization. Certain people are so powerful that they can control your friends, your relatives, and your family by the use of other people. In the past we used to be scared of the Mafia but now there are various types of criminals and it can become very hard to understand their movements and motives. Criminals can use weapons to hurt you, they can use tools to hurt you. They can use poison to hurt you. They can use emotional blackmail to hurt and use you. They can manipulate you and manipulate people that you know. They can use your family to hurt you. They can use your friends to hurt you. They can use your coworkers to hurt you. They can use strangers to hurt you. There will always be people around you who can hurt you for reasons or without reasons. We label those who sell drugs as criminals, as well as those who sell weapons, who steal money from you, or who steal any kinds of valuable things. Criminals can do things and to blame you for something that you have not done. They can be many people coming together to blame you for something that you have not done or even state as official witnesses that you are responsible. It is a way of blaming you even if you did not do the action. They are many people so you have no way to prove that you did not do anything wrong. What is sad is that if you are blame for something that you have not done just because of people who wanted to blame you with false information. In our world, there are many individuals who can be labeled as criminals including those who cause destruction by: bombing, hijacking, kidnapping, murdering, being a thief, use biological weapon, doing sabotage, and committing an assault. People can accuse you of something, blame you for something, and yet they are the true criminals. It is very hard to defend yourself alone when you are surrounded by over 10 and more criminals. Obviously, we will live together by being happy without any kinds of attack. But is it really possible to live peacefully in this world? You be the judge…

# Religion

Having faith in a religion is great, a believing in god is peaceful. God is seen as the most holy; most merciful, the forgiver, the generous, the kind, the most peaceful creation. Depending where you live, you may have a different belief system in regards to religion. One may believe in one religion whereas, someone else may believe in another religion. The most common and popular religions in the world include: Christianity, Islam, Hinduism, Buddhism, Sikhism, Judaism, but there are many other branches and sects of religion. Since the creation of the human species we have evolved day after day. Each religion comes in during a different era with various purposes. If you do not believe in a religion, then you are called an Atheist - an Atheist is someone who does not believe in any religion or god. Some may believe in a super powerful force but neglect to believe in God. Believing in God depends on each individual. Since the creation of religion people have each had faith in something. When you are opposed to a religion you were seen as being inherently against them. People started wars to defend their religion, to defend their beliefs. For many years in the history of religion, you will hear that one area invaded another area just to show their power and worship their religion. People killed people so that they could take part in their beliefs; they wanted to spread their believes by killing and hurting other people. People with different intentions used religion to rule the world; this is how in many countries they share same religion, same beliefs. Some even use the term religion to make money and still we use religion for various purposes. Some sell cloths different foods to portray a religious festival so that they can make money, others sell crosses to remember Jesus Christ. In India we sell statues of various Gods and those who make it make money off of that. Every religion has their own festival, clothes and some holy foods. What is disappointing is that people actually take advantage of people and make money or sell wrongful things to other people. If you take a moment and see how it is important to be believe in something, but in the modern society we tend to believe and we are very philosophical about religion. What is not correct is to harm someone or make him disbelieve in his religion by using of force; by hurting an individual we can make his believe change. We can believe in Islam and many years after we can believe in another religion, hence, we can also not believe in a religion at all. However, it is not correct to use religion to start a war or to hurt someone physically, psychologically, socially or to kill someone outright.

Allow religion to be saint and holy. Believe in any religion that you want - you should have the total freedom.

## Work

Nowadays, finding a job is very difficult. The competition is enormous. We and the majority of people attend school and have a degree for one purpose: to be able to find a job after graduating. The are so many different subjects that we can study and there are so many different types of jobs that we can work in. Some are specialized jobs, while others are odd jobs. Regardless of what job you do, it will bring you money. We live in a world that is productive: the more you work, the more there is chance of making money. Some people even have two jobs. What is unfortunate is when your colleagues at your respective workplace decide to turn against you. We call this Constructive Dismissal. More precisely, the employer or employees behave in a different way with you. They may find details that work against you, look for any mistakes you make in order to blame you. Some even create false rumors to hurt your feeling and to put you down. Others may tell people that you are a thief or that you have stolen something from them, even if this is false. Suddenly, you are trapped and do not know what to do or how to behave with them other even others. You may feel that they do this just so that you can lose face and honor. For someone who works in a customer services base, a client may do anything to fire the worker or even the coworker may do anything to let him or her out of work. It is terrifying to live and to work in that types of condition. Sometimes, you may lose motivation and try to find another job. However, you may not get other jobs because your coworkers or even employer may say or do things just to punish you. Sometimes, the employer may not give you a good reference, hence, you cannot get another job for a certain time-frame. This could be because you did something against them or simply because you are not lucky and they dislike you for personal reasons. Some may even force you to resign, which is illegal and should always be reported and contested. What is the solution one might ask? Usually when your coworkers go against you, you should have discussed it with a supervisor or the employer. It can also be discussed with someone from the human resources department, a doctor, or even a therapist. Explaining your pain is the first step; be open and discuss your feelings and the situation honestly. It is necessary that you take control of your work situation; if you do not control then someone else will control you. Obviously, work can bring stress but you need to be able to manage stress. Regardless of what job you do there will always be a stressful event near you. There are things that you have to let go of and accept the way they are. Moreover, if you see that a certain job can harm you or your reputation then sometimes it is best to change jobs or find a better one. You can also find odd jobs for a certain time and then move on to your field of study or even the job that makes you happy. Remember, never regret it if your employer fires you. There are thousands of jobs outside, it is a matter of simply looking for one. Out of hundreds you will find at least one. Notwithstanding, looking for a job can also be a full time job. The better you search, the better luck you will have at finding the best job. Keep your options open, keep your mind open,and do not refuse to try a different job. The majority of the population studies in a certain field and works in a different field. Some even change careers over time. During early adulthood you may work in a certain field, over time during mid-age you may work in a different field, and while aging you may work somewhere else that you never thought you would. When you look back, you see the changes and challenge the ideas that you had for yourself. The accomplishments that you got during your career will be worth it. Remember: change is good, change can bring a challenge to your life. For some, change can also be difficult, but you have to accept and choose to learn something new. Problems can happen at work but you need to find a solution. With solutions you will find answers to your questions.

## Reputation

In the dictionary, you will find the definition of reputation when you type on the Google search box. Here is how we interpret the word: Reputation as good, great, excellent, bad, stellar, tarnished, evil, damaged, dubious, spotless, terrible, ruined, horrible, lost, literary, corporate, global, personal, academic, scientific, posthumous, moral, artistic. Each word has it own image that can describe more the thousand words. For many people can lose everything but they cannot lose their reputation. Overtime, you will create your name in away that, just by talking about you, people will have an image in their head. Some may say that you are a great person other may say that you are the worst person in this society. Each individual has to build their own reputation, but others will put it high or simply destroy your reputation. By calling you names such as thief, loser, liar, ugly, fat, slow, mentally ill, outcast or simply does not feed in. Other can say good things about you, people like to describe in a nice way to those who like you. Some like to talk good about people. They may feel that by putting you up they might also go up. How nice you were, how gentle you are with people, how talented you are at work or doing something. We like to hear good things about us, it is normal and it is natural. Being reinforced positively is all about reputation. However, negativity can also make you popular. You can become the star due to people's reactions of you, and people can also make you look bad. Reputation does not work alone but works with people. Without mentioning your name, you will not be recognized in society. Some choose to not open up in front of people while others wish to be known. It is disturbing for people to be described as a thief, or a criminal, or mentally ill. People talk about it and some enjoy talking about it just to put someone down even if it is false. Others may plan to put you in a bad spot so that they can record you doing something negative. Some may even have someone videotaped while making an individual drunk and show the community how bad that person is. Others may put up traps such as you being with another women while being in a party or somewhere else and show to your wife or girlfriend or your lover. Hence, as a result your wife or girlfriend decide to breakup. It is fun to some, but disturbing to others and very painful. This may not happen in your community or society but it is happening in other communities and societies. Age is a factor, and gender is also a factor. Your character is a factor just as your honestly is a factor. Your surroundings may have chosen to be cruel to make you look bad. The previous sentences may sound awkward but it happens in real life. Reputation works hand in hand with gossip and speculation. People may be afraid of you or may fall in love with you, it is all about marketing. It all depends on how you polish and shine in front of others. Some may lie to show a better image in front of the society, other may lie to hide their truth. Like we say better the person you know then you do not know. But do not judge people without judging you. Some people will always tell you lies and always tell you the truth, what you should believe in based on you. However, investigate before you doubt. The person with multiple spots may be a very good person and the person who is putting down may have a good reputation but he or she is doing everything to put down the other person. Reputation is like saying Abu Sayed Zahiduzzaman is quite a respectable man. Abu Sayed Zahiduzzaman is well respected around town. Abu Sayed Zahiduzzaman is a man everyone thinks well of. Abu Sayed Zahiduzzaman is a man with a solid reputation. Reputation is more likely your own character. You are in control of you and decide who you are. You choose which religion to worship or not. You chose to believe to be right and what you believe to be wrong. These are all aspects of you and your character. Your reputation is owned by others. You reputation is defined by others and how others talk about you. Therefore, you have to be solid by being critical; that will make your actions that will clearly demonstrate your character. If you want to socialize it is important to have a good reputation. Employers will hire you if you have a good reputation. Build a personal brand in order to create your reputation. After, all your reputation represent your identity - it is who you are at the end of the day.

## Intellectual property

What is Intellectual Property one might ask? In the WIPO website they discuss Intellectual Property. It refers to what you have created or invented such as inventions, a symbol, patent, artistic work, images, literary and name used in commerce. It talks about trademarks, geographical indications and industrial designs. It protects also copyright-based for those who write novels, music, poems, play, films, and create artistic works such as sculptures, photographs, drawings, paintings and architectural design. Your creation comes from your mind; hence it needs to be protected. It is very painful to see that you created something and someone else is getting the rewards. According to WIPO, Intellectual Property was first recognized in the Paris Convention to protect Industry by 1883. Since then it has been well recognized around the world. What you have created should be under your name. When you go shopping or to buy something at the mall or store, it is great to see how many creator or inventors that there are in our world. It is fascinating to admire what has been created by human intelligence, but it is very disappointing when someone else take your work and put under their name.

## Political

If you are male or female and there is an election near by you are wanted to participate in it. You are wanted to run in the popularity contest. You on behalf of other people will run in an election chosen by the population to represent them in a parliament. Like the famous speech says "A government of the people, by the people, for the people" (2017). It is amazing how hard the election can become. The enormous amounts of money that are used for campaigning. It all depends on how you do the marketing for yourself to run against others. The amount of time that is put in to run the election. The people who trust blindly and work blindly for must be outstanding. How talented you have to be in order to get people to support you, to represent you and those who chose to do volunteer work with you. The representative is someone who is priceless and people who support also are priceless. The people who believe in you without even thinking to back up. Politics is something that is very powerful and very complex to understand. In the USA presidential election, you saw how it became nasty and how both party disgraced each other. How painful to see each candidate blaming each other. If you think for once, there will always be people who will criticize you, blame you, put you down for no reason or for any reason that you mentioned to do it. People will always attack people regardless of your status. People will always comment in regards to your voice and idea. You are the head of an area, city, state or province and country, some will follow you until the end, other will fight back to lead you down and other will not take any side. This is how we evolve over time. This is how we become more modern. However, the past can also be extremely modern but we have no sources of seeing their advancement and technology. Hence, present time will always be the right moment. If you cannot run in the next election there will always be room for you to the next one. What is bad and what is good depends on you. Politically, one can do something good and it is seen bad toward you or something bad which is seen as good politics. It's all dependent on you.

## Espionage

In the Merriam-Webster dictionary espionage is described as the "practice of spying or using spies to obtain information about the plans and activities especially of a foreign government or a competing company industrial *espionage*" (2017). In a country where multiculturalism is honored by the government, people and the native people who live in that country are fortunate to live in a western country. We live better then many other countries. People dream to come to our countries. We are lucky to be part of a great system that works. What is important is that we can respect the country laws, people and follow the rules. If people respect what needs to be respected, there is no threat. However, some people go to other countries to break rules, boundaries and to punish others. Some even come to imbalance a country. Why should the government be on alert one might ask? This is when you think about doing espionage. Espionage works both way, you can send your people to sent secret information and your people can betray you by sharing information. Sometimes both may need to collect more information. Like we say "give and take is fair game". There will always be various types of espionage. Some examples are to spy on a country, others a big corporation, or companies, other some extremely dangerous people, other can be to take your invention, other can be to spy your husband or your wife even your children either to protect them or to heart them. Most likely it is to protect innocent people and to live free and to have freedom. For many it is a dream to be part of a secret services. It is honorable, noble and the best no one know that you are honored until you are discovered or revealed publican. Some spy pictures are put in the museum to remember them and to appreciate their work during a crucial time by protecting the nation. Who can become a spy or do espionage? Well, anyone can become one, however, it will depend for what purpose you do it. It is also very dangerous. Your life will be always in a red and danger zone. It is all about wanting an adventure.

## Corporation

It is great be a self employed but what is even great is to have your own corporation or even company. You are the head of your corporation, you make the rules, you make the decisions, you are the main person in charge. Every owner started from a small company and got bigger and bigger with time, until becoming a multi million or even multi billion corporation. Who does not dream to become one or be part of a big corporation? However, not everyone in your corporation will think like you. Some enter to your life, to your mind, to your corporation to do sabotage, to damage your property, to put in the market value down. What is the solution one might ask? You have no choice but to remove them from your company. The last option is to fire them. As a result, some will become your competitors. They will compete against your corporation. Some big corporations chose to buy your small corporation or find way to knock you down by putting your small company under threat of bankruptcy. In certain cases, some companies use espionage to collect your data and information or find out your plan and how you intend to run your business. Therefore, you have no choice to protect your business and it might cost you a lot. Some big corporations buy other corporations to multiply and to run their business. If we did not have employers many of us would not have jobs and we would not have the status that are able to enjoy. We should appreciate our employers and our leaders. After all, everyone does their job. Regardless where you work, you need to respect the employers and the job has to be done nicely and accurately.

## Science

Science is defined in the Merriam-Webster dictionary as: knowledge about or study of the natural world based on facts learned through experiments and observation: "a particular area of scientific study (such as biology, physics, or chemistry): a particular branch of science. It is a subject that is formally studied in a college, university". Science is a way of discovering various new things in the universe and how it works. We study how it worked in the past, how it works in the present and how it will work in the future. Scientists are thrilled to study with facts and data; they are motivated to find the results. Science is also a process of discovery that allows us to find and link the isolated facts by trying to understand the natural world and universe. With science it is possible to develop new technologies, treat and find diseases, and find solutions to various types of problems. Science will be never be finished, it will always find something new. It is continually refining and expanding our knowledge of our universe and galaxy. What is good about science is that people all around our world participate by elaborating on it. Science relies on testing ideas by figuring out what its expectations are, generated by other ideas and other observations to find if the expectations hold true. What is great about studying science is that anyone can become a scientist. You need to apply an understanding of how science works ad affects your life everyday in all sorts; it is fun and is accessible to everyone. However, when talking about science we also need to do experiments in order to find how it effects us and find responses for better ways to help human beings develop. When talking about experiments, humans study humans and human experiments by taking other humans. This is when we harm other humans. For example, we have to study a cure and we need to put in needles and injections to better manage and find solutions to the problems. Hence, some extreme people may use it to harm other humans by injecting poison. Same may do experiments without the approval of the Health Department of their country or even World Health guidelines. This is when it gets out of control and in certain cases we may even create new diseases without find the cure. Therefore, people die everyday as a result of immoral scientific experimentation. Experiments have two sides, one is to improve the quality of human life and the other is to damage and hurt human species by wrongfully using scientific knowledge. Humans around the world are attacked through various illness and we do not know if humans from one country use various types of poison of to spread diseases; they spread death. What is ironic is that when there is a new disease in the market a certain pharmacological companies seem have found the cure within a few weeks to months. It is like they put the problem on the table and show the solution immediately after. If you use science in a proper way, humans will protect other humans and have a better future.

## Cyber Space Attacks

With modern technology we face modern attacks, we call them Cyber Space Attacks, also known as computer attacks. According to the FBI, the most common attacks through the computer are Financial fraud such as (Credit card frauds and Online Gambling), Cyber threats (Theft of information), Cyber Warfere, Drug Trafficking, Cyber Terrorism and extortion, Child pornography and Viruses. Criminals use computers as a target; using a computer to attack other computers or using as Computer as a Weapon; using a computer to commit real world crimes such as Cyber terrorism or even Child Pornography. There are a few types of attack. An example of an attack is Computer Vandalism, which occurs when one tries to damage or destroy data instead of stealing or misusing it. We called them Cyber vandals. It is often used through programs that attach themselves to a file and then circulate it though various computer. Other types of attack can be Virus dissemination. It is used by creating software that will attack your email as soon as you open it or Web Jacking or by Bombing your computer with various files and data. There is also Denial of Service Attacks that files E-mail box with spam mail that fills out your inbox. Some people are gifted with knowledge of Hacking your computer or can even open it with your Password; regardless of what Password you choose they will have to power to open it. Some hackers are even able to access your computer from their computer, and will be able to see and access the information on your computer, including what you are typing or what you are writing or what you are seeing. Statistically speaking, the most costly kinds of attack including: Phishing and social engineering 11%, Web-based attacks 12%, `Denial of service 23%, Malicious code 25% and other types of attack 29%, a total of 100%. Obviously there are other types of Cyber Attacks and there will be new form of attacks in the years coming; the more we evolve, the more different types of crimes will be introduced.

Regardless of the attacks you face, you will always need support emotionally, psychologically, socially and morally. Therefore, meeting with a psychologist or other type of therapist is necessary and urgent. You may face obstacles with finances, you may be trapped in a criminal case, you may be brainwashed religiously, or at work, or someone wants to put a spot in your reputation, or wishes to become you by through a case of an identity theft with intellectual property, some are broken down when they choose politics, or even may face espionage, or you may work in a corporation and you are blamed for something, people can use you or your family for scientific experiments, or you are simply in front of your computer and there is a cyberspace attack against you.

When you go through different types of situations you will feel hurt emotionally. Your mood will change. Either you will show madness or even anger towards your spouse or children or other family members. You will not be able to control yourself because of the pressure that you face. Whereas, psychologically you will be deranged. You may worry about something over and over, you may feel agitated, you may feel more stress due to the situation, you may start having various types of problems. If you already have a mental symptom this may create you more tension and it might affect more your health. Hence, socially, people talk and create more gossip. You will feel bad to meet people who betray you and bad mouth. You will no longer know who to believe. You will loose face and doubt about their honestly. Moreover, morally, you will no longer see the principle of being yourself. You may feel different and see different because of the situations that you are facing it. What is the purpose of being with people who intend to harm you? The only exception are your family members, but even they are to be taken into consideration. Your wife sees you differently, you may choose to stay with her for a certain time but over time your mind may change.

Regardless of the attacks you face, the first doubt can be someone who you love and who you respect the most. Afterwards, you will doubt your friends and then even strangers. Like we say, if there is a robbery at your house, the first person to doubt is your family members first, then your friends and then the strangers. When having robbery in your house happens after many weeks or months of observation, it is usually people that you know as they are the ones who look for information about when you leave home or come home. They know your schedule and they base that on when your house is empty.

What should you do when you face financial problems? You should consult a financial adviser. When you are face with criminal charge you should seek for a lawyer. Religiously if you have doubt you can talk to a priest or even a religious leader. At work you should consult your supervisor or even your employer. If you think that someone stolen your intellectual property see someone specialized in this. Politically can consult a minister of your area to give information or to ask question. Report to the authority if you find someone who is doing espionage. Try to be the best in your corporation. You may get a bonus. Avoid doing experimental design toward other people. Report to police if you find someone doing cyberspace attacks.

## Gossiping, Rumors or Speculation

Gossiping, spreading rumors, or creating speculation is also another form of attack. There are three different types of attack: Personal, Group and Corporative. Personal attacks occur when your spouse, family members, coworkers, friends or even strangers create rumors to attack you personally. This may include: Talking about you to others, talking about your financial situation, illness, or even characters. Making fun of you or how bad you are, or you look, or what you do. The main goal of the attacker is to put you down or to state something that he or she believes in whereas you do the opposite. If a man has cheated on his wife as vengeance, the wife decides to gossip about him toward other females or even his friends and family members, talking about his honesty.

For some it is a ritual, it is normal for a woman to talk about a man or sometimes a man talking about a woman just because the man or the woman is frustrated. You will realize that we talk about someone and the other person shows mercy by taking the time to listen. It is also a form of way of creating a new friendship. People feel closer when they hear bad things about someone. Some people feel for other people when something happens to them that is not acceptable. Some people plan to start a speculation. For example, a man will tell another man "I will talk good about you if you pay me a certain amount of money." Women will love you to hear good comments. "You will find easy a woman because she will state positive comments about you," whereas, if you refuse to pay then people will hear bad comments about you. You will lose face in your community.

The other example is when one mentions to the other, "you talk good about me, and I will talk good about you. You put me up, and I will put you up as well". Like the proverb says; "Give and take is fair game." Furthermore, suffering from bad gossip can also hurt at work. If one is accused of stealing something from the co-workers even though he or she did not, this can ruin his or her career, making someone look like a thief is not good for the person in question or even for the coworkers and the company or organization. Just because some people decided to be against that person does not mean that he or she deserves to be fired. Some coworkers can be cruel or racist; it is typical for someone who never experienced working in a multicultural environment and joint work to see things differently. Therefore, blaming one person can be very easy because we are not used to working with a person who is not the same race and gender as us. Some may have behavioral problems, which can put this reputation in question. It is too easy to blame someone. However, we should put ourselves in question before blaming someone either outside the company or at work. Gossiping, rumors, and speculation can also be cultural.

In modern society, we hear more comments about stars, politicians, actors, musicians, artists, and other famous people. Some are paid to have their pictures on the front of a magazine while others are on the TV or Internet or even talk over the radio. When people start rumors one after another one, the public tends to get used to it. For someone who is very sensitive, these rumors can easily hurt them. It hurts their reputation, their image, and their name. Some may even end up committing suicide. When you have enemies, this can get out of control. Enemies will do anything to put you down, to hurt you emotionally or commit emotional blackmail. They may take a picture of you with someone else and show others, even your wife or husband, "proving" to them that you are not honest even though this may not be the case. The purpose of emotional blackmail is to control you; you will have no choice but to surrender to bad and cruel people.

The world is so small that millions of people can hear about you, see you, or read about you. With modern technology, everything is possible, whereas, within a group it is different. We talk mostly about the group. It can be a sports team, or a representative of the Olympics where someone states that he or she did something against society or violated the law. For example, an Olympic representative has taken steroids before the contest. He or she won by taking illegal drugs. This tarnishes the reputation of their home nation. Because of that, people begin to talk about it. It is normal for some people, while others may find it particularly shameful. Another example is when a political leader has cheated in the election to win. If caught, one may lose his or her reputation and honor.

Corporative rumors begin when people start with negative comments about the corporation to sabotage or damage the company's reputation. Some may share the private information of the company to other companies, and this can affect the company in question. For example, when people use rumors to lower the share in the market, people sell their assets quickly to put a particular company down. In the stock market, people may sell shares, and the value of the company may get lower due to the speculation. Many people may lose money, and some may declare bankruptcy. Losing your savings can be terrible; for so many years, you have saved money, and you invested something that you believed in, and now you have no money left. Companies have lost their market value over time, and some have no choice but to close their doors and lay off their workers, even being unable to give their workers their final salary.

Losing face or hearing negative feedback can be tearful. One should not create gossip, rumors, and speculation for no reason. People are emotional, and many often try to commit suicide after hearing bad things about them. Many feel depressed. For some, it becomes a mental illness. Some depressed patients or people become suicidal. Someone else's life can be under your arms or your mouth. Hence, you should be careful with what you say or do. Even though someone may have done something terrible or face something difficult he or she should have respect and honor. People make fun of people, which can be seen as usual within some cultures, while others may not tolerate it. Gossiping, rumors or speculation can also be seen as verbal attacks. You will end up feeling better to be with people who respect you and talk good about you. If you create a positive environment, you will feel positive, and it will lead you to be part of that group longer and feel better to be part of a great corporation. Be kind to others and others will be kind to you.

As mentioned above, you may face various difficulties, choose a psychologist or therapist or counselor to make you feel better and make you feel like you again.

## What is crisis?

On the Varywell website, the word crisis is defined in the following terms: "In mental health terms, a crisis refers not necessarily to a traumatic situation or event, but to a person's reaction to an event. One person might be deeply affected by an event while another individual suffers little or no ill effects (2017)." When someone is suffering from an obstacle in life, mental or physical, such as: losing a sense of control, having suicidal thoughts, seeing their body changing, feeling fear, confusion, hurt, sadness, powerlessness, failure, and uncertainty, they may begin to show common symptoms. Some may isolate themselves, while others experience difficulties in concentration. A small group of people consume alcohol and take drugs, while some may have mood swings. Others have a problem controlling their anger. A small percentage of people suffer a change of sleeping habits, others in eating, while some even feel fatigue. During crises, you may be feeling as if you are struggling and having difficulties time coping.

## Teen life crises

Every teen lives a different life. The ages of young adulthood can be a confusing time of changing hormones, turmoil and asking difficult questions. Unfortunately, there is no secret recipe for solving every particular situation; each situation is unique and must be addressed accordingly. You need to help your teen in navigating through the hardships and experiences that they are passing through. Your teen's crisis may be different than that of another teen. Sometimes you may feel as if you cannot recognize your child. It is your responsibility to raise your teen and to help them to manage their mental and emotional states better. As parents, we may not know what to do or how to do it. We need advice and helpful ways of getting it including talking to other parents or health professionals. You know your son or daughter better than anyone; do not let your son or daughter tell you differently. Your son or daughter may be having mental health issues, may be abusing drugs, may be consuming alcohol, may be going through depression, or maybe thinking of suicide.

Usually, some teens may skip class, and even some may drop out of school. Regardless of how parents or teachers influence your teen, they have the last word in making their own decisions. It is a transition from teen to adult. Therefore, some teens may think that they can make decisions like an adult. They may do so even if it is the wrong decision. Parents have no choice in but try to make them understand or find a better solution. The majority of teens may not go through counseling; they may refuse to meet a health professional for some reasons. Every day is a drama at home: friends become more important than family members, and some may not have a good relationship with their siblings. Therefore, they feel as if they have to decide for themselves.

Some early signs of mental health issues with your teen include irritability, anger or hostility. One may have a lack of interest in activities and may do poorly at school performance. They may have dramatic changes in eating or even sleeping habits. They may also begin changing friend circle, from an old one to a new one. Teens may have lack of enthusiasm and motivation in everyday routines. They may have thoughts of death or may begin joking about committing suicide. These are the warning signs that you should take in consideration about your teen and all of your children. However, it is also an age of getting involved in sports. Teens will create new groups that will participate in games. Encourage your children to participate in various activities with friends; it is healthy to see them happy and enjoy every moment of their life. It is the most critical time of their life, and they need your support as much as possible. Do not be scared to ask questions; it is the only way to get answers. Ask questions in a calm and caring way. Take the time to get involved and participate in their lives. After all, you are their parents, and they are your children.

## Early adulthood (18-25) crisis

When one reaches their eighteenth birthday, they feel mature; it seems as if one has more responsibilities, and is no longer a teenager. You are ready to face life, but it is also a stage where one does not know what is best for us, despite the fact that we have to decide where we want to be and where we want to go. We begin asking more questions about ourselves, while still spending times at clubs and pubs, listening to music, and spending most of our time with friends. Still, it is difficult not to feel as if you should have already accomplished something, and this often results in an early adulthood crisis. While we may not have all the responsibilities of an older adult, and we will usually live with our parents – with the exception of a few people who decide to move into their own rented apartment – many young adults are attending university or working on their career. Young adulthood is a stage where curiosity prevails; we want to see the world, travel, experience new things, meet new people, and are searching to find what we are passionate about.

One follows the lifestyle that one wants. It is a transition period in which one decides whether or not it is better to stay single or to be with a partner. Some look for a relationship; people discover one's body and want to share his or her body with another partner. It is a time where one may also find themselves struggling financially. Many individuals struggle with not knowing where to spend money or how much should they earn, all while trying to be independent. Some have loans to pay or bills to pay, and they begin to slowly mature financially and become responsible by being independent. It is also a time where we are influenced by our peers, friends, and the surrounding world. It is a time where it is novelty to go for coffee dates and shopping. You may have realized that half of your friends are settling down, getting engaged, and start having families, whereas the other half are stumbling out of nightclubs and enjoying life with different people. It is a time that we may feel as if we are never good enough and try to find out what we like, what we dislike, and begin discovering new interests every day. It is a stage where we learn about ourselves; we strive to be well-rounded, successful, educated and to be empathetic generation.

During your early adulthood you may go through various obstacles and you may have to tackle many of them. Take it one day at a time. Be gentle to yourself. You will enjoy life more if you get as much physical activity as possible. Learn to do relaxation or meditation techniques as well as exercise. If you are having a rough time, try to think preventatively. It is necessary to stabilize the situation before moving forward. If you are having problems at work, notify your boss. Try to control your worries. If you need emotional and psychological support consult a psychologist or counselor. There are many free and easy to access resources that are there to help you. Do not feel shy when looking for help.

## Adulthood Crises (quarter-life crises) 25-35

What are the signs of an adulthood crisis? If you are aged less than 35 years old, and above 25 years old you may be facing a quarter life crisis. It is something that two-thirds of young adults may experience. If you are at this stage, you may be facing a sense of panic in your life and may be facing doubt and questions about your career, relationships, finances, and responsibilities. One may begin to feel doubtful about their own lives with the many kinds of stresses of becoming an adult. It is a period where people may feel lost, anxious and panicked. However, one should not feel alone; many people within that age range are feeling the same way.

You may feel trapped in your body and life, about making the right choice with your job, relationship or both. You may feel that a growing sense that changes is possible if you take the next step. You may feel the need to or may quit your job, or end your relationship for a better change and possibly break your commitments because you feel trapped. You want to redo your life with better adjustments and make better decisions, starting fresh in every aspect of your life with the intention of doing better in the upcoming years.

According to new research by British psychologists, "The study is substantiated by a survey done by Gumtree.com which revealed that 86% of the 1,100 young populations who were questioned admitted pressured feelings to succeed in their finances, relationships, and jobs before turning 30. Two out of five people and approximately 32% felt pressured have their families by the age of thirty. Also, Six percent had a plan to emigrate, while about 21% wanted a complete career change." Many individuals experiencing the quarter-life crisis are often experiencing feelings of being confused, lonely, scared and lost. People do not know what to do or what is best for them. They do not know if it is important to be in relationship or just be by themselves. Many of these individuals need therapy depending what they do. Some go through counseling, while others may not think about living their life the way they want to without going through therapy.

## Symptoms of Midlife Crises.

You may wonder why people change over time; what actually happened to them in their midlife when you turn back time. The following information includes some sign of Midlife crises. First of all, some desire to get a better job by quitting a good job. Seeking out something different. Others decide to do running, biking, dancing, sky diving - basically desire a better physical change with their body. Talking about dancing, some explore new musical tastes. A few people suddenly desire to learn to play a musical instrument. Some men and women show interest in drawing, painting, writing books or poetry. Some may wish to get into physical shape and have toned muscles on their body. When things go wrong some run away from everything. It seems that they fear for problems. Others feel good to get hurt because they have unexpected anger on them. Therefore, when they see into the mirror, some do not recognize themselves. A certain percentage will change to the balance of taking vitamins. People desire to surround with different settings.

You will see some change in people by investigating new religions, churches. Some would color their hair. Some chose either diet or change radically to what they eat. A few group of people may feel some change in their life. Leaving their family or changing partner. Also shifting sleep patterns, some sleep less other more. Men or women chose to restart things, feel like to be part of young crowded. Which could lead to looking back to one's childhood. What he or she missed or would be able to change if they where in the past. Some men and women chose or teach others or become a healer. Those of them tech also by mentioning their experience on success or lost to other. Either due that they recently experience something extremely new or something stressful due to change of job, divorce or death of someone who cared a lot. One is looking forward to get free from problems.

People change over time; time also changes over time. It is always a new hour, a new day, a new week, a new month, a new year and it continue over time. Middle Adulthood is between 45-64 of ages. Typically beginning in the early mid 40, the crisis often occurs in response to a sense of mortality. When people get tired of something they expect new things to come to them: a new expectation, a new desire, a new hope, a new dream and a new breath. A few people desire a simple life, others begin thinking about death. If these situations or problems occur to you then you are going through a midlife crisis and should consult a psychologist or any other therapist.

# CHAPTER 10

# BENEFITS OF COUNSELING

## Benefits of Counseling

One might ask what the benefit of getting counseling or what is the advantage of sharing his or her story with a therapist. Over a period, talking about feelings, emotions, suffering, tension, or what makes one feel blue have been helpful to people. Just the fact that the counselor is there to listen to your problems or to understand you and help you to find a solution is already the first step for achieving better mental states. In the following paragraph, one can read the benefits of counseling. It will help an individual through the next steps: discussing having Less Anxiety, Self-confidence, Better relationship, Regaining emotional balance, Increased assertiveness, Stress relief, Ability to set boundaries, and you may find ways to cope with reality.

## Less Anxiety

When having anxiety, you need to be patient; you need to observe what makes you feel anxious and you have to trust yourself. The therapist will help you to learn more about anxiety, and then he or she will try to identify and recognize your worries. They will then begin the process of classifying your worries, which will, in turn, assist you in finding ways to cope with your situation. Your therapist will begin assisting you in creating a toolbox to allow you to follow a sequence of steps to lessen your symptoms. When you worry, it is a sign that you are a caring person, worrying will lead you to be prepared to solve problems. Worrying can also motivate you to do better and to find a new challenge. However, it is important to feel relaxed and to stay calm when being a counselor.

If you can't, it is fine, as the counselor is there for you, to help you let go of what you have inside of you. You may learn to stay away from the person who is making you feel anxious. If that is not possible, ask that person to stop the behaviors that are making you anxious. If it is due to drugs or alcohol, you need to work on cutting out these addictions while being with the therapist. The main goal is to help you find your way so that you can feel less anxious on your own. Within several sessions, you will find a coping mechanism that can help you to feel less anxious and avoid falling back into an awkward situation.

If you are anxious, find the solution to your problems. It is important that you take a deep breath when feeling anxious, and begin to do things that might help you feel better. Try to sleep well. Tell yourself when having anxious thoughts that these things will go away. You are a better person, and you will do what it takes to make you feel better. Try to create an encouraging statement. For example, "I am a great person, and I am strong." Always look for the positive. Having positive thoughts in your mind is helpful. If you cannot manage anxiety, then no one can manage for you. A psychologist will help you find all the tools necessary, but you have to work on making yourself feel better by being positive and caring for yourself.

Doctors suggest that you spend at least 15 minutes of sunlight a day to boost your mood. Sometimes, depending on the weather using light therapy box can also be helpful, if you are alone trying to slow down your breathing. Try to reassure yourself. Do activities; move around. When working on a task, take your time and, if needed, do it in separate periods with breaks in between; go out. Ask yourself questions about yourself; question your thoughts. Try to see though situation; be a reasonable observer and use your judgment. A counselor won't try to make you mad or make you frustrated; they will try to bring less anxiety toward you. They will be there enough times as to help you feel a release. You will see that a therapist uses short or straightforward sentences to guide and help you to be predictable with your behaviors and thoughts.

# Self-confidence

You will always represent yourself when alone or with people. When things are not going the way you want, life is difficult, especially when what you see is not happening and you do not see yourself up to that level. Hence you need to boost your self-confidence, your self-esteem. It is natural that you sometimes feel inadequate, unacceptable, unworthy, unlovable or even incompetent. We all go through these small phases. It is normal to have negative beliefs or even criticize yourself. Sometimes, if you do not criticize yourself, you will not learn what elements of your life require growth. Hence, live in the moment. Live your life. Live the way that makes you feel good and happy. No one will make you happy if you choose not to be happy.

Let your worries go away and focus at the moment. Create awareness for yourself. Try to find a way to understand your emotions to your actions. It is necessary to respond healthily. For some, writing in a journal or reading books are ways to increase self-confidence. For those who enjoy writing, they may see themselves in what they wrote or what they are writing in the journal. It can motivate a person to see positive words in their mind. Try to be non-judgmental, respect yourself and accept yourself. Find ways to recognize your successes even if you fail on something. There will always be good and bad; sometimes shame and blame change to pride. For certain types of people meditation also help. If you are healthy, then your mind will also feel healthy. Give yourself time; in today's modern society we are overloaded with work. We work more to get money.

People are obsessed with money because it allows you to live the life that you want. Do things in your life so that you can be proud of yourself by participating in your life. Encourage yourself to become active and assertive. Do not keep negative thoughts and feelings in your heart, let them go and practice mindfulness. You have to trust yourself and choose what is best for you. If others do not love you, love yourself since you deserve love. Connect with people who love you. Focus more on being positive. Try not to think about negative talk. Set all types of challenges for your health, mind, and body. Find a solution for what is affecting your self-esteem. In order to improve your self-confidence, you need to know more about yourself. It will make you feel good to dress nicely.

Take control of your life and change negative self-confidence to positive self-confidence. Create a good image for you, an image that people will like to see. See yourself through a mirror and let people see you.

If you cannot talk about your self-confidence to anyone, talk to your counselor. When bad things happen, let the counselor know. Finds ways to reward yourself, such as going out to celebrate a small win. If you feel that something is wrong with your body, then see a physician and change your diet accordingly. Exercise and try to reduce stress. Furthermore, be kind and generous towards yourself. Also be prepared to face any kinds of the situation at all time.

## Better relationship

We all dream of having a perfect relationship. However, in most cases, it is not possible. As the months and years roll on, problems also roll on. Over a period, we seek out patience, gentleness, thoughtfulness, understanding and general common sense with our lover. What happens is that we fall apart or we have no choice but to break out of the relationship. Over time, we assume that our partner knows us well and it seems that everything is perfect. With time we find each person's details and small mistakes which lead to creating misunderstandings between couples. In that situation, you should ask yourself what you want from your partner. Be clear and honest with your partner. If you cannot be honest with your partner, there will be a gap between you. The more you know your partner, the better you can handle your situation. You should become an expert on your partner. You should know your partner physically and emotionally and try to comprehend them psychologically. Try to be creative with your partner, asking the same question over a period of time can become tiresome.

Your partner may not respond you the same way. If needed, paraphrase or rephrase your sentences. This might have an impact when asking your partner questions. We all like to see change, and we all love to hear new things and to see new things. If you lack imagination, create a weekly ritual or series of checklists. Write down what you want to do or even what your partner wishes to do with you. Soon you will see by yourself what needs to be done. Maintain person hygiene, and try to be as attractive as possible to your partner. It is important to keep yourself maintained, as you would appreciate your partner to do. Sometimes it is important to be romantic or flirty if this is the kind of thing that you and your partner appreciate. It is always nice to be gentle and caring. Break out of the dinner and a movie routine, and try to do something different.

Do not forget that kissing, holding hands, and cuddling are vital components of a romantic relationship. If needed, take time off from work. You may need a mental vacation for a while. If your relationship needs fight breaks, then take it. Give yourself some time and some time to your partner. Often, regular breaks can change people minds and allow much needed personal space. You should forget and forgive disappointment, rejection, loneliness, and disrespect if you feel that the love you have for your partner outweighs any fights. When fighting, it is necessary to apologize, as it counts a lot between couples and even friends and family members. If this does not work out, then you should seek an appointment with a couple's therapist. He or she is specialized to help you. Studies show that, in many cases, counseling helps people to overcome issues and to regain confidence and rebuild the hole that was created while going through a difficult time.

## Regaining emotional balance

Often, when being in a couple or while looking for someone, we feel that we have lost the control of our emotional balance. One may suffer from rejection which can activate the same areas of your brain as physical pain. Therefore, it is essential to let go of your painful feelings of rejection. The earlier that you can do that, the better it is for you. If you allow yourself to feel helpless after a failure, you will blame yourself, and you will feel that you were unlucky. It might lower your self-confidence and self-esteem. Even if you fail at something, it is always possible to regain what you have failed. If you keep in your mind your past hurt, you will have the memories replaying in your mind. Feeling guilty is a useful emotion if it stays in the mind. However, guilt can also damage your mind.

The kinder you are to yourself, the better you may be with others. And the more chances there will be to forgive others. If you stay positive and you have positive affirmations, it will can an excellent tool for your emotions and health. A few ways of getting your emotional balance include remaining optimistic. Having good daily experiences will help you to cope by managing your stress. Accept yourself for everything. Tell your conscience that you can do anything and everything. You shouldn't measure your worth by comparing yourself to others. If you think that a person is better than you, accept it. Remember, your time will come someday. Therefore, do not lower yourself. The more you are connected with the society and environment, the more you will know what is going on around you. Always stay connected, and you will meet people who also want to be connected. Some may be in your situation, so do not give up. When something good happens, remember to express gratitude. People who are thankful for what they have been able to cope with stress and various problems do not forget to think about the purpose of living and the meaning of what went wrong. Make it look like a positive situation. Understand and learn your environment. If you are stuck, then talk to a therapist or even doctor. Sometimes the doctor can prescribe low dose medications.

## Increased assertiveness

Through therapy, you can learn how to use assertiveness to your advantage in stressful situations. The more you feel stressful, the less you might be assertive. When some people are not assertive they may fear conflict, may lose a relationship, maybe criticized, or feel rejection. Therefore, the more you go to therapeutic sessions, the better you might be able to solve problems and the better you will be able to face reality. When being assertive, it is important to express yourself effectively as it will make you stand out and look good. Assertiveness is based on mutual respect; it makes you appear to communicate diplomatically. It is direct communication between you and the other person. Those who neglect to have assertive personalities may face passive behavior. Some may feel stress, others resentment, and others seething anger, while a few percentage feeling of victimization and other desire to exact revenge. Emotional balance promotes physical health and is a prerequisite for personal well-being and growth. Your counselor will be able to help you develop assertiveness.

## Stress relief

One way to relieve stress is to use relational response. For some, watching TV is a way to reduce stress, while others enjoy listening to the radio, some enjoy reading, and many prefer the Internet as a way of relieving stress. How can you reduce stress over a period of time? One way is to meditate; a few minutes of practice per day can help reduce anxiety. A deep breath can also help. You should try a 5-minute session first;

when doing something new, do not rush, slow down and be present. Let your body be free. More precisely, do exercise and reach out. Here are the practical natural stress reducers. Try massaging in your body. You can also exercise or play sports such as hockey, baseball, basketball, football or even soccer. If you do not like to exercise but like to play a game, it is better than exercise. One thing for sure which will help you is to eat healthily, and avoid junk foods. Nowadays, people spend more time at home rather than outside. One reason for this is due to the internet and cell phones. People browse through the internet and use their cellphone to play games.

Doctors may also recommend taking B Vitamins; it might help you feel less stressed. A therapist will tell you to avoid Caffeine, alcohol, and nicotine. Try to get more sleep. Try relaxation techniques. Talk to someone that you know if you feel lonely. Take control of your mind and body. Do something so that you do not feel bored. Manage your time, and try to have an agenda for your everyday tasks. Put everything that you are required to do in writing. The more you are organized, the better you can feel about it. Become aware of your stressors. Put positive psychology into action. Avoid toxic people. Get into the right frame of mind. Take care of your body. Better manage your time by cutting unnecessary stressors. Focus on something, and do tasks now instead of later. Remember that there are no problems but only solutions of situation. Discuss how you should find a solution with a psychologist or other therapist. If high stress makes you depressed, take antidepressant medications. Consult a doctor if other therapists cannot prescribe medication. Do what it takes for you to feel stress-free.

## Ability to set boundaries

It is important for everyone to have the ability to set boundaries. If you do not want something, tell them. Do not let anyone touch you unless you want them to touch you. Do not accept physical sex. Fight back if you can, and contact the proper authorities if you are dealing with Mafia or other Criminal Organizations. Try to report these situations to the police. Do call out someone who mistreats you or uses you for various project or purpose. Do not feel guilty when you do say no. Saying no when you mean yes and yes when you mean no is never a healthy habit. Never let people say things to you or in front of you that make you uncomfortable. Put a limit on your time with other people. Do not let anyone abuse you emotionally, especially those in your closest relationships such as your friends or partner. If others do not let you speak up when you have to something to say, speak up, do not be afraid. Accept other people's boundaries. Communicate your limits verbally as clearly as possible.

Define your boundaries as soon as you are able. Use positive reinforcement to make everyone happy. A reward can be as simple as altering the statements' "thank you" or "I respect your decision." Be as flexible as possible with other people's ideas and words. People make mistakes, and everyone is different. Be patient and believe in yourself and allow yourself to believe in other people. You have the power to form your thoughts and opinions. Be intellectual. You have the ability in building your feelings toward a given situation, as are others. You can say yes or no to your friends and to pursue your social activities. You have the power to choose your own spiritual beliefs, as are others. You set the boundaries for all of these. Discuss the importance of establishing limits with your therapist; what is acceptable and what is not, what suits you and what does not.

Regardless of what you decide to do, do it for you. We are all human, and humans have emotions and feelings. Use your knowledge to make things work. If you need support, ask for it or get it. There are many scientists, doctors, psychiatrists, psychologists and qualified therapists and counselors to help you around the world. If you are a student and you see that there is not enough support towards your country become one specialist in your state.

# HEALING THROUGH WORDS

One way to use "Healing through Words" is through Psychotherapy. Psychotherapy is a very large subject with various branches. It is an umbrella with various topics relating to one subject. Therapists usually are psychologists, psychiatrists, doctors, qualified counselors and social workers. To practice, you need to have a license in Quebec, Canada. You also have to be a member and part of the board and association. Apparently, many counselors, out of them, practice in private and some are part of different health centers such as hospitals or even clinics owned by the governments. Some even work in community associations.

Often, to heal, we need medication if we are hurt somewhere. We may need surgery if we are cut somewhere on our body. We may need to put ice or hot water if there is a bruise somewhere. However, with psychotherapy mostly it is done verbally through the therapeutic way. In certain situation, you need to take medication but other situation you may not need to take any medication. The session with the therapists is done verbally using various way of finding a better solution to heal. Sometimes, it is not necessary to use medication; rather you can use meditation or exercise or do sports that can bring your moral and mood up. Mostly, the goal is to boost your mind and yourself.

This book should help you in various ways in your life and with your surroundings. It might give you more knowledge which you may wish to share with others. It might make you more positive to write more from your bottom of your heart. You may have more knowledge about psychotherapy which you may decide to write on a certain topic. Use this book as a tool to understand a certain moment that you had while reading it. Everyone at least will have a crucial moment, and you may have lived your life differently. Hence, this might make you realized about a certain situation that you had in the past or living at this moment. The knowledge might help you in the future. I hope that you had enjoyed the read!

# QUESTION BEFORE SESSIONS

Short-term objectives therapy

_____

_____

_____

Long-term objectives for therapy

_____

_____

_____

Questions to ask my therapist

_____

_____

_____

How will I know if I'm feeling better?

_____

_____

_____

Can I involve the ones loved in treatment? If yes, then how?

_____

_____

_____

# FAQ

**Question:** Who will know my private things I tell my psychotherapist?

> **Answer:** It will depend on where you will go. The therapist may divulge your information to the health department or a crises center or the police if your life is in danger. It also depends on who is the therapist. However, the sessions are confidential.

**Question:** What about payment? Are the fees covered by insurance?

> **Answer:** If you go to a health center that is covered by the government, in Quebec, Canada it should be free. But if you go to a private clinic to see a psychologist you may have to pay a certain fee from your pocket. Depending on your insurance company, it might be covered, or you may have to pay. Sometimes it is half by your insurance and half from your pocket.

**Question:** What are your fees?

> **Answer:** Depending who is the psychotherapist, the amount may start from 25$ to 100$ for 45 minutes' session to 50 minutes' session. The fees vary from one therapist to the other.

**Question:** What information will be asked when I contact you to inquire the first appointment?

> **Answer:** Usually, the medical secretary or the receptionist may ask your name, address, phone number, medical card number, which doctor or psychologist or counselor you want to meet, and may ask to describe your situation briefly.

**Question:** What information will you give me when I call to schedule the first appointment? What happens in psychotherapy? What can I expect?

**Answer:** One may ask you to explain what is happening in your life; a short description of your health condition and why you want to meet a psychotherapist. You may get good feedback from a professional. The main goal is to make you feel better and to expect that you will recover from your health condition.

**Question:** I am feeling somewhat depressed (or anxious), but I am not sure that psychotherapy is meant for me?

**Answer:** After a few sessions with the therapist you may tell if the session if good for you or not. However, it might take many sessions to recover, and there is no deadline in recovering. The therapist may recommend meeting a doctor so that he or she can prescribe medication for antidepressants.

**Question:** How do I know if my psychologist is the right one?

**Answer:** If you read chapter 6 and 8, it should help you to answer your question. However, there is no right or wrong therapist. It all depends on how you will interact and how deeply you want to recover. Hence, if you do not like a counselor, you may request to change it or see another psychologist.

**Question:** What makes psychotherapy successful?

**Answer:** The answer is simple; it is "Healing through Words."

**Question:** Your websites mention training. Will my therapist be a trainee?

**Answer:** Before becoming therapists there are legal and medical requirements for degrees and licenses that a psychotherapist need to have. Whereas, before taking your medical file the therapist may ask you if you mind being counseling from a trainee, however, one will supervise.

**Question:** How can I make an initial appointment?

> **Answer:** When you feel ready and when you feel that you need medical advice from a health professional. It is a matter of calling to set an appointment or to present in person.

**Question:** What are cyber psychology and psychotherapy with virtual reality?

> **Answer:** It is done electronically by messaging or texting with a computer, tablet or cellular.

**Question:** I have other questions. Who can I talk to?

> **Answer:** Call the crises center or present to the hospital or clinic. If it is urgent go to the Emergency or find a therapist virtually.

# References

*Ilana W. Rosen, MSW (2017).* Turning Point CT.org Retrieved from http://turningpointct.org/story/rachel/

**Merriam-Webster (2017).** Psychotherapy | Definition of Psychotherapy Retrieved from https://www.merriam-webster.com/dictionary/psychotherapy (n.d.) (2017). Retrieved from www.goodtherapy.org/learn-about-therapy/issues

**Wikipedia (2001-2006).** Chess History - ChessHere.com Retrieved from www.chesshere.com/resources/chess_history.php

(n.d). (2005-2010). **TELL: Therapy Exploitation Link Line** Retrieved from therapyabuse.org

**(n.d). (2007-2017).** Drama Therapy Retrieved from https://www.goodtherapy.org/learn-about-therapy/types/drama-therapy

Mahaney. E. (2007). Theory and Techniques of Feminist Therapy - GoodTherapy.org Retrieved from https://www.goodtherapy.org/blog/theory-and-techniques-of-feminist-therapy/

**(n.d). (2015).** Freud, Sigmund | Internet Encyclopedia of Philosophy Retrieved from www.iep.utm.edu/freud/
"Naturalistic Epistemology," by Chase B. Wrenn, *The Internet Encyclopedia of Philosophy*, ISSN 2161-0002, http://www.iep.utm.edu/, today's dat

**(n.d). (2005-2017).** Hypnotherapy - Hypnosis - WebMD.Retrieved from
www.webmd.com › Mental Health

(n.d). (2017). **Psychological & Educational Services Centre**
Retrieved from http://www.ccpeweb.ca/en/services/psychotherapy/
definition-psychotherapy/

**Weilert. L. (2014). Ten Most Common Reasons for Seeking Help from
a Therapist or Counselor**
Retrieved from kchealthandwellness.com › Library of Articles
Tyrrell, M. & Elliott, R. (2003). Uncommon Knowledge Ltd. Retrieved
from http://www.uncommon-knowledge.co.uk/psychology_articles/
psychotherapy.pdf. Rubinstein, N. LMFT, LMHC, (2008). Therapist
in Olympia, Washington.

**Ten Most Common Reasons for Seeking Help from a Therapist or
Counselor**
Retrieved from kchealthandwellness.com › Library of Articles

Weilert, L. MSW, LMSW (2013). Kansas City Health & Wellness
Magazine Retrieved from http://kchealthandwellness.com/ten-most-
common-reasons-for-seeking-help-from-a-therapist-or-counselor/

Howes. R. (2008). Fundamentals of Therapy #1: Who Goes? | Psychology Today
Retrieved from https://www.psychologytoday.com/blog/in-therapy/.../
fundamentals-therapy-1-who-g...

**Fertel. M. (2017). The Marriage Fitness** Audio Learning System
**RETIREVED FROM** https://marriagemax.com/mc2
John. M. (2016). PsychCentral.com Retrieved from https://
psychcentral.com/lib/7-reasons-to-seek-marriage-counseling/

(n.d). (2017). HuffPost Lifestyle Retireved from http://www.huffingtonpost.
com/2014/06/02/marriage-counseling-_n_5412473.html

Pearon. C. (2017). **This Is What It's Like To Be Young And In A Sexless
Relationship...**Retrieved from www.huffingtonpost.com/2014/.../sexless-
relationships-young-people_n_5492962.ht...

Sicinski. A. (2017). R**How to Overcome Hurt and Start Moving on with Your Life** Retrieved from http://blog.iqmatrix.com/overcome-hurt.

River. O. (2017). **Signs of a Midlife Crisis - Personal Tao,**
Retrieved from *https://personaltao.com › Personal Tao Teachings › Midlife Crisis & Transformation*

Eoc Institite (2017).
**The Power Of Music Therapy - Meditative Sound Healing Audio Retrieved from**
Ad*www.eocinstitute.org/.*

(n.d). (2017). Wikipedia **Music therapy**
Retrieved from *https://en.wikipedia.org/wiki/Music_therapy*
(n.d). About Narrative Therapy - the Narrative Therapy Centre
Retrieved from www.narrativetherapycentre.com/narrative.html

White. S. (2010). Naked Therapy | Sarah White Therapy
Retrieved from sarahwhitetherapy.com/naked-therapy

PCIT. (2017). **What is PCIT? - PCIT International**
Retrieved from *www.pcit.org/what-is-pcit1.html*

Haherty. J. (2016). **Psychodynamic Therapy | Psych Central**
Retrieved from https://psychcentral.com/lib/psychodynamic-therapy/

(n.d). Relationship counselling and support for couples and individuals...
Retrieved from *https://www.relate.org.uk/relationship-help/ help-relationships/relationship-counselling*

Caplan. T. (2017). **Montreal Therapy | Anxiety | Family | Couples Therapist -**Retrieved from *tomcaplanmsw.com/therapy/*

Dr. Betito. L.(2013). **About Sex Therapy - Syndicated Radio Host...**
Retrieved from www.drlaurie.com/about-sex-therapy.html

Dr. Chow. V. **Sexual Health Therapy Montreal - Saint-Laurent | Montreal...**

Retrieved from https://www.psychologyresource.ca/.../
sexual-health-therapy-montreal-saint-laurent/

(n.d). (2017). Psychology Today, **The Social Therapy Group, Clinical Social Work/Therapist, Brooklyn... Retrieved from** *https:// therapists.psychologytoday.com › Therapists › New York › Brooklyn*

River. O. (2005-2017). Signs of a Midlife Crisis - Personal Tao Retrieved from https://personaltao.com › Personal Tao Teachings › Midlife Crisis & Transformation

Gausepohi. S. (2017). **Workplace Harassment: How to Recognize and Report It** Retrieved from *www.businessnewsdaily.com/9426-workplace-harassment.html*

(n.d). (1991). **Positive Solutions - Workplace Bullying** Retrieved from *www.positivesolutions.com.au/workplace/workplace-bullying.html*

Chatwell. C. (2017). **Workplace Strategies for Mental Health - Harassment and Bullying...** Retrieved from *https://www.workplacestrategiesformentalhealth.com/.../ harassment-and-bullying-prev...*

(n.d). (2017). **Harassment - Preferred Solutions Inc.** Retrieved from *https://preferredsolutionsinc.com/services-for-corporations/ harassment/*

(n.d). **What is Intellectual Property - WIPO** Retrieved from *www.wipo.int/edocs/pubdocs/en/intproperty/450/ wipo_pub_450.pdf*

(n.d). (2017). Stack Exchange Retrieved from https://english.stackexchange. com/questions/298077/a-government-of-the-people-by-the-people-for-the-people

Brainy. Q. (2017). **Government of the people, by the people, for the people, shall not...**

Retrieved from *https://www.brainyquote.com/quotes/quotes/a/abrahamlin101395.html*

Merriam-Webster. (2017). **Espionage | Definition of Espionage by Merriam-Webster**
Retrieved from https://www.merriam-webster.com/dictionary/espionage
Understanding Science. 2017. University of California Museum of Paleontology. 3 January 2017 Retrieved from <http://www.understandingscience.org>.

(n.d). Types of Attack **Images of all types of attack**
Retrieved from *bing.com/images*

Hite S, (2000), Shere Hite Sex & Business, p. 3-4, retrieved June 13th 2015. United Nations (1997-2010). What is sexual harassment. *Women Watch*. Retrieved from: http://www.un.org/womenwatch/osagi/pdf/whatissh.pdf

Rubinstein. N. (2008). LMFT, LMHC, therapist in Olympia, Washington. Retrieved from https://www.goodtherapy.org/therapists/wa/olympia

*Ilana W. R, MSW (2017).* Retrieved from http://turningpointct.org/story/rachel/
Hill. A. (2011). The quarterlife crisis: young, insecure and depressed | Society | The...
Retrieved from https://www.theguardian.com › Society › Depression

Quinn. L. (2015). **Trying Out Adulthood: Why The 'Early 20s Crisis' Is Definitely A Thing** Retrieved from *elitedaily.com/life/culture/the-early-20s-life-crisis/1224740/*

Juneau Suicide Prevention. (2017). Retrieved from http://www.jys.org/11-warning-signs-your-teen-is-in-crisis/

Distance Education. (2011). **Teenager Crises Causes | Counselling | Intervention | Adolescents**
Retrieved from *https://www.acs.edu.au/info/psychology/counselling/adolescent-crisis.aspx*

Bockarova. M. Ph.D. (2016). 4 Ways to Set and Keep Your Personal Boundaries | Psychology Today Retrieved from https://www.psychologytoday.com/.../4-ways-set-and-keep-your-personal-boundaries
Cover and back pages designed by « Khalid Hussain (Shaheen)

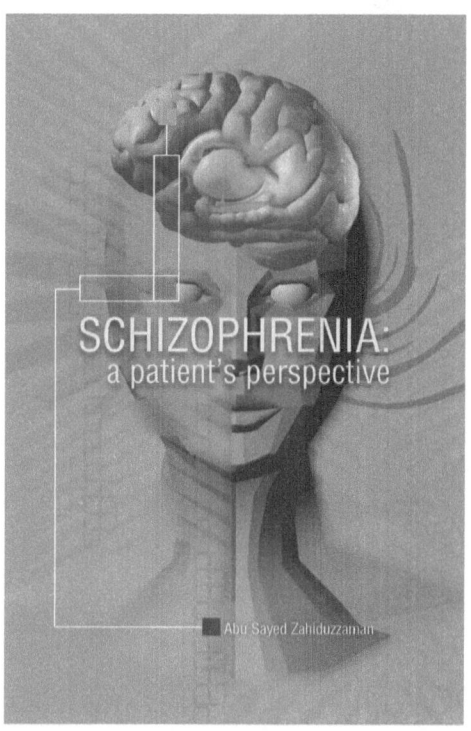

Schizophrenia: a patient's perspective

This book will enhance your knowledge and change your perspective on mental illness. You will have a better idea on how to cope with someone who has a mental illness. This book not only talks about depression, psychosis, and schizophrenia but gives and idea on various aspects of life and learning. One will learn some stories and theories that I have developed and experience while I was hospitalized. This book contains 88, 490 words I hope you will explore to the fullest.

Abu Sayed Zahiduzzaman graduated with a degree in Bachelor of Arts majoring in Psychology from University of Windsor, Ontario, Canada in 2003.

Author: Abu Sayed Zahiduzzaman

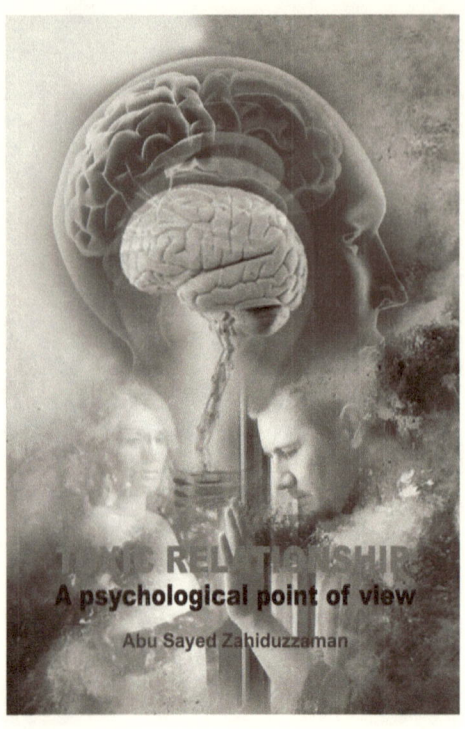

Toxic Relationship: a psychological point of view

This book, Toxic Relationship: A Psychological Point of View, might give one hope, a sense of understanding and learning on how they should behave with difficult relationship. It will help individuals make proper decisions during difficult situation with people that they were about. This book covers various topics on toxic relationships between family, work, friends, and also discusses some of the theories that the author has developed regarding these topics. After reading this book, the reader will have a global knowledge on toxic relationships and hope to cope with them. The book will help the readers realize that they may not be the only ones going through hardship. The author of this book discusses various types of situation that can occur between boyfriends, and girlfriends, husband and wives, friends, colleagues, brothers, sisters, mothers, and fathers. It covers relationships in details and also discusses separation and divine.

Author: Abu Sayed Zahiduzzaman